TRUST FUNNEL

TRUST FUNNEL

LEVERAGE TODAY'S ONLINE CURRENCY TO *GRAB ATTENTION*, DRIVE AND *CONVERT TRAFFIC*, AND *LIVE A FABULOUS WEALTHY LIFE*

BRIAN G. JOHNSON

NEW YORK

TRUST FUNNEL
LEVERAGE TODAY'S ONLINE CURRENCY TO GRAB ATTENTION, DRIVE AND CONVERT TRAFFIC, AND LIVE A FABULOUS WEALTHY LIFE

Published in New York, New York, by Morgan James Publishing. Morgan James and The Entrepreneurial Publisher are trademarks of Morgan James, LLC. www.MorganJamesPublishing.com

The Morgan James Speakers Group can bring authors to your live event. For more information or to book an event visit The Morgan James Speakers Group at www.TheMorganJamesSpeakersGroup.com.

Awesome Web Marketing is not affiliated with Google, Amazon, Facebook, or other companies that may be featured within this book. All trademarks belong to their respective owners.

A free eBook edition is available with the purchase of this print book.

CLEARLY PRINT YOUR NAME ABOVE IN UPPER CASE

Instructions to claim your free eBook edition:
1. Download the BitLit app for Android or iOS
2. Write your name in **UPPER CASE** on the line
3. Use the BitLit app to submit a photo
4. Download your eBook to any device

ISBN 978-1-63047-297-9 paperback
ISBN 978-1-63047-298-6 eBook
ISBN 978-1-63047-299-3 hardcover
Library of Congress Control Number:
2014941739

Cover Design by:
Chris Treccani
www.3dogdesign.net

Interior Design by:
Bonnie Bushman
bonnie@caboodlegraphics.com

In an effort to support local communities, raise awareness and funds, Morgan James Publishing donates a percentage of all book sales for the life of each book to Habitat for Humanity Peninsula and Greater Williamsburg.

Get involved today, visit
www.MorganJamesBuilds.com

Habitat
for Humanity®
Peninsula and
Greater Williamsburg
Building Partner

CONTENTS

ACKNOWLEDGMENTS

To my wife, Amanda, I love you, and I'm blessed to call you my wife. Thank you for the support, friendship, and love in both good times and bad. Thanks to my dad, Gary Johnson. I'm grateful for the relationship we share today and the times we have spent together, like the crazy and silly road trip we took to pick up the one and only Otis!

To my mom, Judie Johnson, you were a firecracker, a woman who lived life to the fullest, and an amazing role model. I'd like to think you'd be pretty darn proud of how I've lived my life over the last fourteen years. I love and miss you.

To my best friend, Otis, thanks for all the adventures, hugs, and love.

In business, I've always done a good job at surrounding myself with winners—that is, those who are playing the game just a bit better than me. It's allowed me to get to where I am today, and I am thankful and grateful to so many. Thanks to Joel Comm for the friendship and guidance; thanks to Colin Theriot, Kevin Rogers, Justin Quick, Laura Natasha Catella, and other gifted copywriters who I've had the pleasure of working with over the years. Thanks to Tim Castleman and Andy Shepard for guidance when it comes to business relationships. Our talks have helped me grow. Thanks to Ken McArthur for giving me a shot and introducing me to so many wonderful people. Big shout-out to Rick Butts, who helped me shape this book and come up with some fun hooks we'll explore soon such as "the seven-minute syndrome."

Thanks to E. Brian Rose and his partners, Bryan Zimmerman and Chad Casselman at JVZoo.com, for creating such a great digital selling platform. Thanks to my coding partner, Danny Ramdenee, for crafting some of the most elegant and powerful plugins and scripts. You make my job easy. Thanks also to Vio Bancui and Mario Soto Jr. for helping with various projects and being part of my community.

Thanks to Aidan Booth for being such an amazing student, partner, and friend. Watching your journey has been my privilege. Thanks to Alex Goad for the mentorship over the years. You taught me much about sales and conversions, partnership and more, and I'll always consider you my friend.

Thanks to Matt Cutts at Google for keeping me on my toes and always thinking.

Thanks to many of the joint venture partners I've worked with in the past including James J. Jones, John S. Rhodes, Matt Rhodes, Rachel Rofe, Keith Dougherty, Martin Wales, Jason Fladlien, Wilson Mattos, Steven Clayton, Tim Godfrey, Mark Ling, Brad Callen, Matt Callen, Daniel Hall, Ross Carrel, Bryan McConnahea, Jonny Andrews, Sara Young, Ben Shaffer, and so many others.

Thanks to the following individuals that have inspired, educated, and shared their wisdom over the years: Kim Garst, Tina Spriggs, Donald Wilson, Mike Carraway, Lori Ruff, Ben Adkins, Brian Horn, Kate Bush Jr., Brad Gosse, Chuck Mullaney, Lester Lim, Ben Littlefield and his partner, Dr. Dan, Zsuzsa Novak, Stephen Renton, James Schramko, Michael O'Neal, David Perdew, James Malinchak, Sean Vosler, Dan Nickerson, John J. Cornetta, Tom Beal, Kathleen Gage, Brad Spencer, Lisa Gergets, Valerie Duvall, Nicole Jolie, Warren Peterson, Seth Larrabee, Darren Monroe, Amber Ludwig, Daven Michaels, Tony Laidig, Tanner Larsson, Ron Douglas, Mario Brown, Matt Gill, Ken Ster, Mike Filsaime, Andy Jenkins, and Paul Clifford.

Most of all, thanks to the tens of thousands of people who've purchased my products over the years. Know that it's you that motivates me and keeps me moving forward day to day. Thanks for all the friends and followers on Facebook and other social sites. Lastly, thanks to David Hancock, Rick Frishman, and Morgan James Publishing for picking up and publishing *Trust Funnel*.

There are many others that I've been blessed to cross paths with; if that's you, I thank you.

FOREWORD

By Joel Comm

Trust. It's not something most people give easily or take lightly. Sometimes trust is built in unorthodox ways—like the happenstance way in which I came to know and work with Brian G. Johnson.

A number of years back, I received an email from a man named Brian Johnson. He wanted to introduce me to a new information product he had created and asked if I would be interested in sharing it with my readers.

I'd known Brian for a number of years and didn't think twice about saying yes to him. After all, he and I already had a relationship, and I trusted that whatever he was creating would bring value to my readers.

Only after I had shared his product with my readers (and generated some very nice affiliate commissions as a result) did I realize something important: This Brian Johnson was *not* the same Brian Johnson I was already friends with! Oops. We had a good laugh together, and Brian explained that while he was grateful that I shared his product, he was surprised that it was so simple to get me to say yes.

Since the time I made the incorrect assumption that all Brian Johnsons are the same person, I have gotten to know Brian G. Johnson. He has demonstrated again and again that he is all about creating and nurturing healthy relationships with others by delivering value in all that he does.

So was it serendipity? I suppose so.

The thing that made Brian's initial product so valuable was his understanding of creating value, driving traffic, and converting prospects to customers. I've seen him do it again and again through a variety of products and services he has created over the years.

If you've ever had the opportunity to meet Brian, you'll know that his molecules bounce off each other faster than many of us are accustomed to. His high-energy personality translates well to his live presentations, where his karate kicks and animated gestures integrate well with his message.

That message is that *you can build your own business and achieve great success by working at home in front of your computer.* His strategies and techniques have helped many others take steps toward living their dreams, and I believe he can help you as well.

In *Trust Funnel*, Brian channels the best of his online knowledge and passion to help others into a practical guide that is both informative and easy to read. Packed with useful illustrations, actionable strategies, and a healthy dose of Brian's sense of humor, *Trust Funnel* will teach you how to run a simple online business that can provide you with the lifestyle you've always wanted.

Go ahead. Jump into the funnel and see what comes out the other side. I think you're going to like it.

—**Joel Comm**, *New York Times* bestselling author of *The AdSense Code, Twitter Power, KaChing, Click Here to Order* and *So, What Do You Do?*

ONE-CLICK CASH MONEY

If you've ever wanted to quit your nine-to-five, have more time and financial freedom, work for yourself, and ultimately live a fabulous life as an online entrepreneur, this book is for you.

Trust Funnel is based on well over eleven years of full-time experience with *driving traffic* and *converting that traffic* into money by generating the sale of a product or service online. These two components are the cornerstone of many online success stories, including my own, and they are also the focus of this book.

HOW TO DRIVE TRAFFIC AND CONVERT IT INTO MONEY

Never in the history of the world has it been easier to establish a simple moneymaking business, thanks to the Internet, yet so many struggle to achieve life-changing results. In fact, according to the A.D.D. marketing group, well over 95 percent of all Internet and affiliate marketers fail to make any money, according to a recent study.

Here's the good news: Success leaves clues. In fact, not only does success leave clues but it provides a clear path forward, allowing *anyone* willing to take action a chance to live the life that so many people dream of but never realize.

Success is not about being the smartest guy (or gal) in the room, it's not about being the first to discover the "perfect opportunity," and it's not about having the best tools for the job (although great tools certainly don't hurt). Rather, success is about assessing opportunity, creating a plan of action to achieve a desired outcome, and prioritizing daily efforts to meet that goal.

Trust Funnel will pinpoint why so many fail and *what to do about it* by providing insights that can only be gained by time spent in the trenches. As we move forward, I will address common issues that stop many from achieving their dreams and goals.

The pages ahead will provide more than just "how-to" information; they will walk you through what to do, when to do it, and why. The content of this book will put *you* in control of your own destiny, which is paramount for success.

However, you won't be going it alone. *Trust Funnel* will guide you through the process of establishing a critical component of any successful online venture: your own marketing site.

I'll be here to ensure the process is simple and easy. I'll show you how to use the free CMS (content management system) platform WordPress to launch and install your website. Furthermore, with this book you will also have access to video training found at my own marketing site, MarketingEasyStreet.com.

WHAT'S A TRUST FUNNEL?

Trust Funnel is a play on the phrase *sales funnel*, which is used to visually outline various offers that a prospect is presented with during the sales process. A sales funnel can be incredibly simple, where the prospect is presented one offer, or it can be quite complex, with multiple buying opportunities presented as a prospect moves through the sales process or funnel.

A well-constructed sales funnel is a powerful tool that can greatly improve overall earnings for both product owners and affiliate marketers who earn commissions when generating the sale of the product. For this reason, marketers tend to focus on creating high-earning funnels while often neglecting other critical elements that can significantly impact and improve earnings. A sales funnel, while important, is *one singular component* that contributes to the overall success (or lack thereof) of a product launch—and ultimately a thriving online venture.

Over the years I have watched as various product vendors successfully launched and leveraged complex sales funnels that yielded amazing earnings, not only for the vendors but for the affiliates who promoted the products—only to see incredibly high refund rates weeks later due to an inferior product, lackluster support, or other issues that plagued sales.

This outcome leaves vendors and affiliates scratching their heads, wondering *where's my money?*

I've also witnessed marketers work on incredible products for months on end and finally reach a launch date that produces subpar results due to a lack of targeted traffic.

Traffic is the most critical success element; no traffic equals no sales.

When it comes to online sales and marketing, it's incredibly easy to lose sight of the human element. Vendors and affiliates quote sales statistics such as EPCs (earnings per click), often forgetting that it's *people* that are buying.

As we move forward, we'll explore the **big picture** when it comes to Internet marketing. You'll learn simple yet powerful tactics in SEO (search engine optimization), list building, persuasion, self-publishing, video marketing, and lots more all focused on those two critical elements—traffic and conversions. This will allow you to drive traffic and generate sales of your own products or other people's products as an affiliate. It will allow you to enjoy that fabulous life I mentioned earlier. Furthermore, I'll help you to identify what to focus on, in what sequence, and why.

Let's begin with a quote:

> *"If people like you they'll listen to you,*
> *but if they trust you they'll do business with you."*
> **—Zig Ziglar**

That's powerful stuff touching on three important factors:

- Like
- Trust
- Business

Years ago when Mr. Ziglar shared his enthusiasm for sales and motivation, he certainly wasn't thinking about the Internet and online sales specifically. However, today trust *rules* when it comes to ecommerce, and it does so in multiple ways.

Here's another powerful quote that I'll return to often:

"People listen to those they like and buy from those they trust."
—Unknown

Trust has become one of the predominant, if not *the* predominant, factor in all areas of online marketing. Trust powers the Google search algorithm. Facebook's entire platform is based on the "like" button (liking someone or something is a precursor to trust), and it's not just Facebook that has adapted a voting system based on likes. YouTube, Reddit, StumbleUpon, and similar sites empower users by allowing them to decide what they like and what they don't. When these sites see content that is liked and well received by their user base, they further push out that content to even more of their users.

Today it's the **users** who decide where the traffic flows and what products are bought and sold. The whole ecommerce paradigm is based on a fundamental sales factor that has been in play for thousands of years: trust.

In the early years of the Web there was no Facebook, Twitter, Google+, or Pinterest. There were no viral videos or YouTube, and the term *video marketing* was years away. If you wanted traffic, chances are you were leveraging SEO.

Google based its rankings on an archaic computer program or "algorithm" that was easy to fool. The ranking system was based on links, which are still important to this day. However, the game has changed drastically. Now, Google also takes into account likes and trust, and without these items, great rankings are no longer possible.

What is old, the trust factor, is once again new.

TRUST FACTOR—THE EASY WAY

Let me also mention this: Build trust and you won't need to sell. Merely recommend products or services, and you will earn. If you do decide to roll up those sleeves and sell, you will be amazed at the kind of response you will be able to generate. In fact, let me go on record and say that when I've rolled up my sleeves and put together a great product and offer, the results have been staggering.

Trust either works for or against Internet marketers, just as it impacts sites like Amazon.com, Zappos.com, and other leading shopping portals. This book will guide you through the process of launching and leveraging any web property that has been optimized to build trust, drive traffic, and make money—a Trust Funnel. Please understand this is not about trickery or black hat Internet magic, but rather smart marketing strategies that will yield results for the long term.

AN ENTREPRENEUR IN THE MAKING

Ever since I was a teen, I dreamed of working for myself. The word *entrepreneur* was not in my vocabulary back then, but I knew I wanted to call the shots and not have to answer to others. Working like that just seemed more exciting and rewarding. In order to achieve my desired goal of not answering to "the man," I tried all kinds of cockamamie ideas and schemes to make a buck.

I failed, then failed again, then tried once more, and continued this cycle for many years. This trend of always trying various tactics and strategies and failing often would serve me incredibly well in the years to come.

My earliest memory of a personal computer is when my dad purchased a shiny new Apple IIe in the early eighties. It didn't take long for my brother and me to discover video games. I was hooked.

However, what really blew me away was what I discovered several years later—the Internet and specifically what it would become in the years to follow. I knew it would completely change how and where people spent their money. People love "easy," and the Internet would provide just that.

But what was super exciting was that I knew the Internet would *level the playing field for average folks, allowing them to cash in as it reached the masses.* To this day I can remember the thought of being able to tap into a worldwide network of people on a shoestring budget. This is what makes the Internet different from all other forms of advertising and media.

I hustled and learned about SEO; I launched site after site, targeting subjects that were commercial in nature. That is, I built sites around those products and services that people purchased online, including web hosting, Halloween costumes, used textbooks, cookware, posters and prints and more. Within months, I began to generate sales and the money flowed. Honestly, it seemed almost *too* easy.

Ultimately I became an online coach and mentor, teaching others how to make money online, just as I had done before them. I realized my calling was figuring out how to get results with online marketing and then teaching others to duplicate my success.

That's pretty darn amazing for a guy who had miserable grades throughout school, got into a ton of trouble (boys like fire, and I was no exception), and struggled with spelling and grammar (still true to this day). In fact, in early grade school some of my teachers mentioned "dyslexia" to my folks. I'm not sure if I have dyslexia or not, but I will say that I struggle with many of the telltale signs.

The magic began in 2002, when I was in charge of the catering department at General Mills, creating meals for the company's big wigs. It was a very challenging job. On busy days I could be running as many as nine or ten catering events, often happening at the same time. I was never one to complain about a challenge, but what really disappointed me about the restaurant business was that often I felt like a cog in the wheel, never being truly appreciated for my effort—and as you may have heard, the pay is less than stellar.

By this time I had been online for several years and had leveraged the Internet in a number of ways to make money, the first of which was multilevel marketing (MLM), or network marketing. However, I disliked the fact that with most traditional MLM opportunities, the norm was to seek out friends and family and then pitch them on the opportunity the MLM offered. I hated pitching to folks that were not really interested, but that's where I discovered the power of the Internet.

By launching a simple website, people who were seeking out information on MLM opportunities *could find me*. Think about that for a minute. Instead of bugging people who had no previous interest in what I was pitching, I launched a website focused on a topic and interested individuals would discover me!

KA-BOOM!

Selling is not hard when people seek out what you're offering. In fact, you don't have to sell much at all but rather give people what they want and they will buy. We'll return to this simple concept of "giving people what they want"— something I like to refer to as the golden rule of Internet marketing—again and again as we proceed through this book.

Around this same time I began to learn about affiliate marketing and improving my SEO. Affiliate marketing is an incredibly simple business model that rewards affiliates (those that sign up with various companies and their affiliate program) with commissions based on the sale of a product or service. Sales are tracked to each individual affiliate by using "cookies" that store data on a user's computer. An affiliate simply links to a website such as Amazon.com, BuyCostumes.com or other online sites that offer an affiliate program with a special coded "affiliate link." Any web surfer who clicks this special link will be tracked to the responsible affiliate. If that web surfer should buy a product or service, the referring affiliate would get paid a commission.

Think about that for a minute! You sign up to an affiliate program—very easy. Then you use a specially coded link that tracks all the traffic you send to a merchant site like Amazon, eBay or BuyCostumes, and if anyone buys, you get paid. Even more exciting is that anyone can get started on a shoestring budget! With clarity I knew that's what I should focus on and prioritize my efforts around. That last sentence is very, very important, and I'll cover *focus* and *prioritizing* more as we continue as well. Affiliate marketing would allow me to go mainstream. I could create websites on so many different topics and target consumers who were searching for products and/or services. SEO and affiliate marketing were and still are to this day a match made in heaven.

I had set my sights first on SEO. I figured *without traffic*, the greatest affiliate offer in the world would not make a bit of difference. So I began to regularly show up on WebmasterWorld.com. You can still find my posts back from 2002 as "Chef Brian." I asked lots of questions, took lots of action, and started to see increases to my website traffic. Let me add here that when I got really serious, I put the money part *out of my mind.* My first goal was simply to learn SEO and be able to drive traffic. Once I accomplished that, I would then focus on affiliate marketing and go commercial.

I launched a website that focused on cooking and recipes; this allowed me to easily create content, as I knew the subject well. Fortunately, my SEO proving grounds were far less competitive than they are today. Not too many folks were trying to rank for "shrimp scampi" or "homemade chicken noodle soup" back then. My traffic ramped up in record time, and within months I was driving as many as five thousand visitors a day from free Google search traffic.

By 2003, it was time to go commercial. I had the skills and knew how to drive traffic on a shoestring budget. My future was bright, and I was filled with excitement. Back at WebmasterWorld.com, I was answering more questions about SEO than I was asking, and I had also launched my first serious affiliate marketing sites targeting posters and prints sold at Art.com.

I remember learning about famous painters like Vincent van Gogh and Pablo Picasso. I wrote articles and targeted keyword phrases such as

"Picasso Blue Period" and "Picasso's Rose Period," and I linked to Art.com with my special coded "affiliate link" and sure enough, the sales came quick and often!

I quickly learned the importance of an "upsell" (a purchase add-on or upgrade) when I discovered that my commissions increased by as much as five or six times when someone ordered a frame *with* their poster or print.

Art.com was the first company to send me life-changing income. I can remember seeing checks for several hundred and then, within several months, four figures. As a professional chef earning around $30K a year, an extra grand or two a month was huge. What makes Internet marketing so very powerful is that you can craft messages (videos, blog posts, Facebook updates, podcasts, and more) based on what people are actively searching for (help them find what they want, and give it to them).

There is no need to push your message onto people with little or no interest. Instead, you can find out what others want, publish content around that very thing, and those folks will find you.

SEO allowed me to do just that and earn that life-changing income. In fact, in 2003 I launched a website targeting Halloween and earned more than $20,000 based on maybe fifteen hours of work. Over the years I targeted dozens of affiliate offers and launched websites specifically to drive traffic focused around various product phrases. I also dipped my toe in CPA (cost per action) marketing and earned well over $100,000 with the AdSense program. CPA and AdSense are additional ways of generating income based again on *driving* and *converting traffic.*

In those heady days of early Internet marketing, I can remember the excitement I felt just thinking about the possibility of SEO and affiliate marketing. I did my homework, studied, and, most importantly, took *lots of action*. I never lost focus, and the results came.

I can recall just months earlier showing up to my chef job and sharing my excitement. Most of my coworkers thought I was crazy and slightly stupid, asking, "Why would you spend hours working on that website stuff when you're only making a few dollars a day at it?"

Some of those folks even laughed as they asked me. However, I had the last laugh months later when I put in my two-weeks' notice and shared once again my excitement for what the Web offered to *anyone* who was willing to take action.

Again, because this is important: I *focused, prioritized,* and *took action,* which later paid off in a huge way. I had achieved the American dream, and I was just getting warmed up.

TINKER, TAILOR—TEACHER, TRAINER

For the next several years I did my SEO and affiliate thing, launched lots of sites, and continued to make amazing money, especially for a "D" student. I lived the life that people dream about— I made six figures each and every year, worked when I wanted, how I wanted, and with whom I wanted. I took awesome vacations, checked into the best hotels, and ate at the best restaurants. The best part is that I worked about three to four hours a day, four days a week.

However, by 2008 I had grown bored. I needed to learn something new, and I wanted to take my marketing to the next level. By this time I had amassed some pretty amazing results. I had launched hundreds of websites, drove an insane amount of traffic, knew WordPress like the back of my hand, and had achieved what so many were looking for: freedom, money, and the life I wanted.

I thought it would be fun to share my ideas and tactics about SEO, WordPress, affiliate marketing, and driving traffic by creating my own information products (which I would sell) based on these very subjects. It was something I had never done, and I love to tinker, tweak, try new things, and challenge myself.

That last sentence is pivotal to what motivated me at the time, and it's how I live my life today and what makes it fun. Before we move on, let me share with you my mantra, the thing I live by: **To help people achieve success online, have a ton of fun in the process.** This allows me to live the life I dreamed about as a child, and it can be your life as well!

And this is where *Trust Funnel* really begins. The year 2008, when I set out to learn *sales and marketing* at a higher level, marks the point when I began to find my voice and audience; when I learned how to create content that added value and made me money at the same time. Most importantly, this is when I started to establish and build trust with those who found me online—complete strangers who would later become customers and friends.

Before I move on, I want to mention that while I began to teach subjects like SEO, WordPress, and affiliate marketing, the strategies and tactics found in *Trust Funnel* can be applied to numerous niche markets. Many of my highly successful peers leverage strategies similar to those found in *Trust Funnel,* yet they operate in very different markets.

The bottom line is that the strategies and tactics found within this book can be used in numerous online ventures to drive traffic and turn that traffic into earnings.

Prior to this time I had sold other people's products, which is very different from selling your own. I found out what people wanted, such as "ghost Halloween costumes," launched a website based on that very search term, linked from my website to the merchant site via an affiliate link, and that was that. The merchant sites paid me an affiliate commission based on the sales generated from the traffic I sent them.

My visitors never knew who Brian was, so I didn't have to worry much about establishing credibility or trust. I let the merchant site I was affiliated with (like Amazon.com) take care of that.

In 2008, I launched my first product called *Revenue Domains Exposed*, a simple PDF ebook and a dozen or so accompanying tutorial videos. It was an information product that was fairly easy to create and launch.

I taught strategies I was using myself to earn thousands monthly by leveraging expired domains to easily drive traffic, which I then converted into earnings with the AdSense and eBay affiliate programs.

As I created the product I also blogged about many of the tactics and strategies I used on one of my websites, creating a three-part series called "Revenue Domains" that was very popular. By the time I published the third post in the series, I had built up trust in the concept and the product. I had shared lots of valuable content with my readers and created a good amount of buzz around the product I would soon be releasing.

This was guerrilla marketing at its finest as it was free, created desire and interest, and ultimately generated well over $5,000 in earnings within the first week of the product launch. Even better, I offered value to anyone reading my blog regardless of their decision to purchase with me.

I didn't know it at the time, but these blog posts were the beginning of my own personal Trust Funnel. Over the years I've continued to release free tutorial-based content in the form of videos, blog posts, and Facebook updates that grow trust, and my customers (I like to call them "members") purchase from me again and again.

Furthermore, all this content led to lots of *traffic*, again a must-have ingredient to online success. Even better, it didn't cost me a penny. When my first product was released, I had immediate sales with no big launch, JV partners, fancy or expensive sales copy, or video—ka-BOOM!

Let me mention that at this time I had a very reasonable goal: just to launch a simple product, that's it. I did not bite off more than I could chew. This philosophy has served me incredibly well and has alleviated information overload as I simply focused on a few core goals. It's also kept me moving forward on the path of learning and success.

Just as I had done when I started with SEO, my goal was only to learn traffic generation via SEO and that was it. I put money out of my mind and began to tinker, test, and optimize my tactics. Once I was driving thousands of visitors a day for search terms like "pan-seared tuna" and "quick and easy chicken recipe," I then began to focus on the money, and it came with ease.

One step at a time I focused on the skills needed to get the results I was after. Since 2008, I have released a lot of products that I'm very proud of, and I've earned well over a million dollars. As I write this, my wife and I are building a custom dream home with a million-dollar view of Pikes Peak, which stands proud at fourteen thousand feet overlooking the city of Colorado Springs. Small steps taken over a period of time can add up to amazing things for those that stay on track.

With each new product I focused on learning and implementing something I had not done before, such as a monthly membership, higher-priced coaching programs, more complex sales funnels, sales videos, new ways to drive more traffic and leads, higher earnings for partners, and more. Along the way, I built my brand, found my voice, and continued to build trust with my customers. Ultimately I learned about selling online and how to get incredible results, working primarily as a one-man operation with the help of an assistant and various partners. Today I continue to focus on things I have yet to do in my online marketing, and I take one step at a time. I've never before released a physical book with a big-name publisher such as Morgan James Publishing, but you're reading the results of that goal right this moment.

Trust Funnel is for **anyone** who wants to earn life-changing income online, whether you're just starting or you've been at it for a while but want to take your marketing to the next level.

WHY I WROTE *TRUST FUNNEL*

Today in the Internet marketing space, I hear so much about links, plugins, new scripts, WordPress themes, and *things* that promise easy traffic and earnings. I hear affiliates asking for the *one thing* that can help them achieve financial success.

People are looking for the *very best opportunity* to help them move forward. They want the one thing that will ensure their success, but they're looking in all the wrong places.

In my humble opinion, there never has been nor will there ever be one single *thing* that can guarantee results. People are looking for that very best method, coach, mentor, system, or strategy, and oftentimes they're leaving out the one critical item that can help them to achieve the success they're after: themselves.

I see so many people who are unsure of what to do and how to do it. I see people living in fear of making mistakes and wasting time—so many amazing people who have so much to offer, feeling as if they're not good enough or smart enough to get things done.

I see people playing the search engine optimization game like it's 2003 by equating Google rankings with "building more links," and while building links is important, it's only part of the traffic equation. With this book I will give you the entire success recipe, allowing you to identify what's important and prioritize all the success factors.

So many people spend time on things that will never help them to achieve the success they're after. This is *exactly* why I wrote this book, which is based on tactics and strategies that have allowed not only me but numerous students to achieve a high-level success.

Trust Funnel is more than a one-trick pony that promises big money with ease. Rather, it will provide a thirty-thousand-foot overview of what I consider *key critical areas* of success, including mindset, philosophy, step-by-step technical details (or "how-to" instruction), and more.

There is no time to waste. Let's get started changing your life for the better.

CHAPTER 1

THE RABBIT HOLE
AND THE RED PILL

Internet marketing is incredibly complex. Each and every day new opportunities, websites, software products, content delivery solutions, marketing strategies and tactics become available by leading experts in the industry. The sheer volume of content that's being published to the Web in the form of tweets, posts, updates, videos, emails, and more is staggering.

In my opinion, this is one of the biggest fail points for so many struggling individuals, often leading to the "seven-minute syndrome," which unfortunately stops many great people from ever achieving anything truly life changing.

The seven-minute syndrome robs people of reaching their full potential. The onset of this disease is so subtle that it's hard to notice early on, yet after a period of time the disease sets in and almost always ends in failure, loss of confidence, and frustration. Those struck by it become unsure of what to do and/or how to do it.

Those with the ailment second-guess themselves, starting and stopping project after project but never reaching the end of anything and thus failing to ever *create assets* that can lead to the success they are after.

Those who have been afflicted by the seven-minute syndrome waste their days away with seemingly harmless tasks that never add up to anything, daily activities that might look something like this: Their day begins as they press the magical power-on button, and as waves of electricity course through their computer, they're excited by the potential of what the day may bring. As their computer monitor lights up, they think, *How about posting a cute picture of my puppy dog or cat to Facebook to wish all of my virtual friends a good day!*

They grab their smartphone to take that cute picture of their puppy or cat, but after snapping a shot they realize the lighting is all wrong and so they move outside to take yet another picture. After the picture has been taken they think, *It would look so much better on Facebook in a nice frame, and it also needs to be cropped to have the biggest impact.*

With that, they open up software to crop the picture and also find and download a software app that will allow them to frame it. By this time they have wasted seven minutes of their day, seven minutes forever gone.

Next, they open up their email to find a message from the self-proclaimed president of Internet marketing, Mr. Frank Kern. Since Frank is *el presidente*, they feel compelled to read the message. Frank's also a lot of fun!

Frank mentions a simple but incredibly powerful strategy for making money online, and they find themselves watching a very cool and highly produced video featuring clips of not only Bruce Lee but Keith Richards too. How could anyone not be drawn in?

By the end of the video, the afflicted individual has spent another seven minutes online (probably twenty, as Frank is really good at this marketing stuff). It's time they will never get back, time that never ends in the creation of an asset.

Even worse, Frank inspires them with a new marketing idea, leaving them asking *should I be doing that and if so, how?*

Next they notice an email from a friend with an awesome viral video featuring "the greatest freak-out" ever. Another seemingly innocent seven minutes gone, never to be regained, never leading to anything worthwhile, and leaving the scoreboard to read a big fat "zero."

This activity pattern often continues for weeks, months, and even years. As time passes, the afflicted individual begins to doubt themselves, wonders if anyone really makes money online, and becomes jaded and distrustful— especially of marketers selling "how to make money online."

Where once they had a belief system that anything was possible and they could succeed, now it is replaced with the need to see proof of results, as skepticism and doubt begin to rule their lives.

CHOOSING THE RED PILL

Let's stop and consider an alternative to the above scenario. What if success was not found in the latest $2,000 product being sold by a leading marketing guru but rather in *how you spend the first two minutes in front of your computer each and every day*?

What if the *success* answer was so simple it was actually hiding in plain sight right in front of you? What if I told you that very average people, with average intelligence, were achieving extraordinary results by simply identifying *what it is they want* and what they *need to do* to get it, and even better, what they absolutely *must have* to achieve their desired goals and dreams? And what if success was attainable by anybody regardless of race, religion, creed, social status, income, and knowledge of the Internet and marketing (or lack thereof)?

What if success really was that simple?

In the 1999 science fiction movie *The Matrix*, the human population is reduced to nothing more than mere batteries controlled and operated by robots that harvest the human race for their heat and energy output.

One of the leading characters, Morpheus, offers a young computer hacker by the name of Neo the choice of picking either a red pill or blue pill, adding, "You take the blue pill, the story ends, you wake up in your bed and you believe what you want to believe. You take the red pill, you stay in Wonderland and I show you how deep the rabbit hole goes. Remember, all I'm offering is the truth, nothing more."

Neo takes the red pill and swallows it.

This scene is so incredibly powerful and represents that Neo, *for the first time in his life*, is in control of his own destiny. He wakes up and discovers he's actually floating and being kept alive in a pool of what looks like Jell-O, with cables attached to his spine. His limbs are weak, and he strains to open his eyes as he's never used them.

Neo learns that he has not been *living* on planet Earth as he thought but that he had been kept alive and living inside the Matrix, a prison created for his mind.

TRUST FUNNEL

Up until this point in his life, Neo has never—not once—been in control and has simply been a pawn in Wonderland. He's never made a conscious decision or created a plan of action allowing him to achieve anything truly rewarding.

Today so many people are drifting through life having never created their own plan of action, one designed to move them toward their dreams and goals doing the things that make them happy.

Rather, they simply drift from this to that, focusing on what's immediately in front of them, doing various tasks and never stopping to identify if the tasks can help them achieve their overall dreams and ultimately make them happy.

Paulo Coelho wrote:

Esther asked why people are sad.

"That's simple," says the old man. "They are the prisoners of their personal history. Everyone believes that the main aim in life is to follow a plan. **They never ask if that plan is theirs or if it was created by another person.** They accumulate experiences, memories, things, other people's ideas, and it is more than they can possibly cope with. And that is why they forget their dreams."

Just as Neo lay still in that pool of Jell-O, never making one decision for himself but ultimately being fed by a computer program, so many people who want success with Internet marketing never really stop and assess the very best plan of action *designed specifically for themselves* which would allow them to achieve their dreams and goals.

It's truly madness.

Instead they are drawn by bright shiny objects like moths to a flame. They are victims of the seven-minute syndrome simply because day to day they have no given purpose, or if they do it's based on someone else's plan for them.

No surprise then that so many folks start and stop projects and often never finish anything. They buy into a program, and once the excitement wears off—once the real work begins—they quit.

It was never really their plan of action to begin with.

The choice is yours.

Choose the blue pill and stay in Wonderland, being entertained in seven-minute increments, never making your own plan of action, which usually leads to little if anything worthwhile.

Or make a conscious decision right now to choose the red pill and craft a plan that will help you focus day to day in the coming weeks and months to create assets that will drive your business.

I can remember back in 2011, while speaking in Vegas in front of about one hundred people, and some of the folks in the audience giggled when I mentioned that I didn't have a Twitter account. In fact, at the time I didn't even really use Facebook or any social media sites. Yet I was standing onstage and had the success that so many wanted.

Even as I write this, in the fall of 2013, I still don't use my Twitter account as I have yet to *focus on it and prioritize it*. However, the things I do use day to day push my business forward and have become powerful assets that I can leverage at any time.

These items include my mailing list. On any given day I can email my list and drive more than one thousand people to any offer, to any sales page, blog post, or Facebook update—that's a true asset. Or I can upload a video to one of my YouTube channels with hundreds of subscribed users and get my message or offer in front of lots of eyeballs. Or I can post to my blog and leverage the trust and authority I've built up with Google to easily rank in the world's number one search engine, again getting my message in front of lots of interested people.

Success Tip:
*Successful marketers march to the beat of their own drum; they break their own path and lead the way. They identify what they want, what they will need, and what they absolutely **must have** to achieve their desired goals. They have a vision of what their business or venture will look like in the future, and they focus and prioritize their daily actions, which allows them to move forward and get results.*

"First comes thought; then organization of that thought, into ideas and plans; then transformation of those plans into reality. The beginning, as you will observe, is in your imagination."
—Napoleon Hill

One of the things that has helped me achieve the success I enjoy is that I don't move forward with something until the last project I started has become an asset, one that can be used to drive traffic or convert that traffic into money.

This book is structured to take you through these steps. First, you'll launch your marketing website based on my SEO formula using WordPress. Once you've completed that task, you will have created an asset. Your site will have the ability to drive traffic from Google, and you'll be able to push and convert traffic from other sources such as YouTube, Facebook, Amazon, and more.

DO I REALLY NEED TO CREATE A WEBSITE?

Note, as we move forward, I'll use and interchange the terms website, marketing site, and marketing blog in the same manner. They all mean the same exact thing—a website that you control, one that is built with blog software (WordPress).

Allow me to ask you a simple question: How many high-level Internet marketers can you name that don't have their own marketing blog? If you're just getting started, you might not know a lot of big-name marketers and thus may not be qualified to answer that question.

Allow me to cut to the chase: Nearly everyone who is making significant life-changing income has their own marketing blog or website.

Of course there will always be a small percentage of marketers who are making money that do not have their own blog. However, so many positive reasons exist for why you should have your own marketing blog or website:

- Free targeted traffic via Google
- Ability to build a mailing list
- Ability to create a sales page
- Ability to point people to a short, memorable, and easy-to-spell domain

As we move forward, I'll guide you through the process of establishing a marketing blog that looks great, is optimized for Google rankings, and addresses the needs of your future visitors.

With that in mind, I simplified and streamlined search engine optimization, and I promise you this: If you can follow a simple formula, you'll be able to publish content that both Google and your future site visitors will love.

In fact, all the strategies and tactics found in this book have been streamlined, simplified, and prioritized for you. I am a massive fan of understanding what's most important and focusing only on that.

When it comes to achieving the success you're after, you don't have to understand how everything works to generate results; rather, you simply need to identify what's most important and focus on that.

Take airplane travel, for example. When you step inside a plane and sit down, do you really understand how the plane works? Can you describe how a plane is able to catapult itself through the air at nearly 800 miles per hour?

I certainly cannot, yet I've flown many, many times and always reach my destination in a timely manner. Learning is incredibly important; however, it's easy to go overboard and spend more time learning than actually doing. We won't make that mistake.

Next, you'll get the opportunity to call the shots and create your personalized plan of action that I mentioned earlier. If you're just getting started and you're unsure, I'll provide a blueprint you can use to make an educated decision—but you'll still be in charge.

You might decide to focus the majority of your time on video marketing and YouTube, or you might desire to tap into the billions of people who use Facebook each and every day. Or perhaps you may prefer to focus and prioritize your efforts toward SEO or self-publishing in order to leverage Amazon. Eventually you will want to use a number of these methods and Web properties to get your messages in front of more people and to diversify your traffic.

With your own plan in place, before you sit down in front of your computer and press that magical power button, you'll already know what you want to accomplish. You'll have a plan of action that has the power to move you forward and get results for you just like it's done for me and countless others.

Having a true plan of action makes all the difference in the world. Suddenly emails from marketers will seem less important. While you may still upload those fun pictures of puppy dogs and cats to Facebook, you will have balance in your day-to-day activities and won't fall victim to the deadly seven-minute syndrome.

Before we jump in and start talking about technical issues like registering domain names, selecting the best Web host, and installing your WordPress site, it's important that we take a look at the mindset as well as the philosophy in which you will move forward with your business.

✔ RECAP:

- Do not suffer from seven-minute syndrome.
- Create and stick to a plan of action that is tailored to you.
- Remember that, for most people, multitasking is a myth.
- Keep it simple; simplicity is powerful.

"Everything should be made as simple as possible, but no simpler."
—Albert Einstein

CHAPTER 2

CREATING A SUCCESS PHILOSOPHY AND MINDSET

Y ou did it. You swallowed the red pill. So now you're ready to commit to something new, something bigger than you've ever done before, something truly life changing. And it all begins with *mindset*.

Your own personal Trust Funnel is established on the philosophy through which you contribute to the Web, deal with customers, interact with joint venture partners, and conduct yourself as you run your business.

The decisions I've made have shaped my business and ultimately led to the philosophy that guides me day to day. You may want to apply some of these principles for yourself as you move forward or use them to shape and guide your own ideas about how you live.

KNOWING YOUR STUFF AND SHARING YOUR SOLUTION

It all starts with knowing your stuff and sharing your experience with your online audience. If you want tremendous results, you're going to need to put out tremendous content. At its core, Internet marketing is all about publishing, and the better the content you publish the better your results.

There's no faking it (though I'm amazed at how many try).

Note, this does not mean you need to be perfect, with a track record of generating millions online and years of results to speak of; rather, it means you need to create products that you know can have a dramatic impact for the better on anyone who puts the methods, strategies, or tools you provide into use.

It's as simple as that. As you continue on your journey you will gain momentum, have more results to speak of, and gain more tactics and strategies to share.

For so many, this is the hard part. They feel as if they don't have anything worthwhile to share. They're not smart enough they reason, nor do they have results that warrant sharing their experience to help others.

This could not be further from the truth. Everyone on this earth is created with a special set of talents, skills, abilities, and passions that make them one of a kind, and to go through life *not* sharing that talent and helping others is a waste. Furthermore, over time, sharing your own life experience, both good and bad, helps you to grow and become a better leader and marketer who makes a long-lasting impact.

It's human nature to come up with reasons why you're not ready, capable, or in a position to share. If the thought of putting yourself on camera, telling a personal story, or speaking in front of hundreds of people is outside your comfort zone, know that this is where the magic happens.

WHENEVER POSSIBLE, SIMPLIFY AND PRIORITIZE

Before we get started, I want to stress two important items that have helped me and countless others.

1. Understand that Internet marketing at its root is very complex, confusing, and overwhelming, especially for people just getting started.

Once you understand this, you can prioritize and simplify your workflow on the *most important* elements that will *bring success*. This allows you to push past a roadblock that stops so many people, or what I like to call *analysis paralysis*. At its heart, Internet marketing is a publishing business; thus it's absolutely critical to *publish* assets that can have a positive impact on your business.

However, if you're second-guessing your every move, if you're wondering about one hundred possible elements that Google puts into its algorithm before publishing a blog post, if you're worried about every small detail that could play into your Kindle book, it will slow you down time and time again.

For example, let's take a closer look at search engine optimization and how it could impact a blog post you're about to publish. Google has mentioned that it takes into account more than one hundred factors when it ranks Web pages online.

Based on this fact, some people might think it makes sense to create a checklist of one hundred factors that Google would possibly take into account so that when they publish anything to the Web they can analyze their content to ensure high rankings.

I mean, can you imagine how crazy that would be, analyzing a five-hundred-word article with a checklist of one hundred items to ensure proper rankings? This is where simplifying and prioritizing your actions on a *daily basis*—focused around the outcome you desire—is so incredibly powerful and will help you to achieve results at a high level.

Here's a tip: Highly successful Internet marketers are very prolific and publish assets time and time again. As we move forward, I'll share with you the formulas and step-by-step processes I've used to simplify, prioritize, save time, and, most importantly, move forward toward the end goal: publishing assets.

2. Play your hand.

In life we're all dealt a hand to play. Some people get better hands than others, some folks are great at bluffing, others have years of experience, and still others are rookies. What's important to understand, however, is that anyone can win—it's simply a matter of putting yourself in the game and playing your hand to the best of your ability.

With time, anything becomes easier. Skills are gained, experience is garnered, and confidence is boosted. It all begins with jumping in and getting started. Let's look at some examples. Let's say that you wanted to lose weight and at the same time thought it would be great if you were able to make some money online. So you researched some niche markets and found that FOREX (foreign currency exchange) software sells incredibly well; it's a niche with lots of consumer demand, which drives sales.

You figured it would make sense to go where the money was, so you launched a marketing blog targeting FOREX, posted comments about various software products (which you really didn't understand), and struggled to drive traffic and make sales. At the same time, you were also focused on losing weight so you started exercising regularly, tweaked your diet, and focused on eating healthy foods to reduce your caloric intake, and as the days passed, you lost weight.

This is a classic example of what I see happening time and time again. So often there is a disconnect between what people publish to the Web and the content of their own lives, which offers a tremendous amount of information to share.

Let me ask you: Would you like to buy a product that teaches you how to make money by leveraging the foreign currency exchange platform from someone who has no practical experience on the subject?

Of course not!

Perhaps you think you don't have any experience or insight to offer that would allow you to make money online. In my experience, this is usually the furthest thing from the truth, but fear stops so many people dead in their tracks.

Don't let that happen to you!

Here's a real-world example of what I'm talking about: At a speaking event in Vegas, I asked the attendees if they had a dog. The room lit up, and most of the folks raised their hands and shouted "Yes, I have a dog!" I then asked those with their hands raised, "Have you ever taught your dog a trick?"

Once again the hands shot up and many people yelled out, "Yes, I taught my dog many tricks!" Finally I asked if they had published a blog post or uploaded a video or perhaps even created an informational product about "how to teach your dog tricks."

Not one hand was raised. Even though so many in attendance (150+) that day had lots of practical experience when it came to teaching a dog tricks, not one person had tried to share their expertise on the Web. That's such a shame because dog training is a huge market, with tons of money to be made. While those folks in Vegas may not have the experience or platform that Cesar Millan enjoys, they have something that Cesar will never have: their own unique life experience, perspective, and skills when it comes to training dogs.

Furthermore, while lots of folks love Cesar Millan, they would also welcome additional training and tactics from anyone who has practical life experiences they could share on the subject. What I have learned over the years is that people love *real*; they crave guidance from those who have already done it. This is more important in my opinion than a perfect website, sales message, scripted video, or advertisement.

It's natural to strive for perfection, and when we think of selling information or creating content that will educate others, very often we think we need to act "professional." That was certainly the case for me when I got started. My first posted videos to YouTube were expected, typical, and incredibly boring. As the years progressed, I loosened up and embraced the sense of humor and antics that make up Brian G. Johnson, which in fact gave people a chance to get to know (and trust) me better.

THE VERY BEST YOU

What I learned at the time was that I needed to become the very best Brian G. Johnson that I could be. I needed to embrace my silly quirks, antics, and humor from time to time while also prioritizing my message—after all, I was teaching people search engine optimization, how to convert traffic into sales as an affiliate, and Kindle marketing strategies. People did not show up for my jokes; however, if I could address their wants and teach them while also entertaining them, it would be a win-win (and also a lot more fun for everyone).

After all, if you could learn the same life-changing tactics and strategies from two different people, one being very serious and stodgy and the other making you smile and laugh from time to time, which would you gravitate toward?

This does not mean you need to brush up on your jokes and incorporate props into your marketing. Rather, it means you should embrace *who you are* and strive to be the very best you!

If you're serious, you will then attract the serious folks out there wanting to learn whatever you're teaching; if you're extremely analytical then embrace those numbers and the numbers folks will find you.

In the previous example about FOREX and weight loss, it would have been just as easy to launch a blog or online journal about the desire and journey to lose weight (rather than foreign currency exchange). The benefits associated with launching such a journal-type website or blog are numerous:

- Publicly sharing your goals and desires means you're far more likely to achieve those goals.
- Content creation becomes far easier when you're creating content on a subject you know like the back of your hand and when it's also the thing you're experiencing. There is no need to manufacture content; you just share the good and the bad. By sharing your story and experience, you

will draw others interested in the same subject to you, making traffic generation, list building, and ultimately making money online much easier (remember: people buy from those they like and trust).

- The ability to impact the world on a positive level and ultimately help people is a tremendous gift, and by sharing your journey of weight loss you can connect with and touch so very many.

Perhaps you're wondering, how can I possibly blog about weight loss when I'm twenty-five pounds overweight? This is a great example of how to play the hand you're dealt! All that is needed is the truth and your life experience. The first blog post might read something like:

Hello and welcome to my blog. My name is Brian, and this is where weight loss gets real! All my life I've struggled with my weight, eating healthy, and getting regular exercise. However, with the launch of this website that's all about to change, and you're invited to experience the ride with me.

While I may not have a doctorate in health and fitness, and I'm certainly not an exercise junkie, what I can promise to share with you are real-life examples of how I'm improving my life by eating healthy, exercising, and striving to lose the pounds.

I'm prepared to share the good, the bad, and the ugly as I move forward with this life goal to lose weight and get healthy. I'd love to hear from you as well, so feel free to comment on the various blog posts found on this site.

This type of journal blog can be applied to nearly any niche market including Internet marketing, learning to play guitar, how to care for and train a dog, and more. It's all about sharing real-life experiences. In Internet marketing, people like to call it a "case study"—marketers love fancy terms.

When I learned I had alopecia (a hair loss disease), I created a blog that generated thousands of dollars by driving and converting traffic. I turned to my favorite holiday and sold costumes, again by driving and converting traffic via affiliate marketing.

When it came to creating my own products I shared the very tactics and strategies I had personally used to get results.

THE GOLDEN RULE OF INTERNET MARKETING

Stated simply, the golden rule of Internet marketing is *find out what people want, and give it to them.*

Sounds so easy, yet people mess this up (because they don't know better) all the time. It's about identifying the wants and needs of your future site visitors and customers and giving them what they're after. This golden rule is really two items wrapped up into one.

- Find out what others want
- Give it to them

Let's take a deeper look into both of these critical items.

1. Find out what others want

It's incredibly important to know and understand what motivates others to take action. In the summer of 2013, I launched a coaching program called Revenge of the Affiliates. Sales of this program were driven primarily by live webinars over a five-week period. I asked the audience at the beginning of each webinar:

What is the single most important thing to you when it comes to Internet marketing, and why did you show up this evening?

Truth be told, I already knew what the majority of the audience would answer with:

Money—to learn how to make money online.

And with that I began the webinar by mentioning that the entire focus of the next ninety minutes would be how anyone can make money online.

Next, I told them what they would learn was based on proven and effective strategies I had personally developed, tested, and tweaked over a twelve-month period, allowing me to earn passive income via the Kindle opportunity without having to write a single word or overcome technical hurdles.

What I did was set expectations and address the number one motivating factor for the attendees—making money! I then addressed additional items that lead to great sales conversions.

The second item I addressed was credibility. I did this by saying I had "personally developed, tested, and tweaked what I'm about to share with you over a twelve-month period." Lastly, I mentioned that my results were achieved without having to write a single word of text—another huge point with my audience.

I was giving the audience what they wanted—a simple way to make money online—while also building up expectations for what would follow. As the webinar progressed, people got to like me, know me, and trust me, and that leads to sales.

This is part one of the golden rule: giving people want they want. I understood what my target demographic wanted and I told them what they wanted to hear first thing. However, I had yet to "give it to them," which is the second part of the golden rule.

2. Give it to them

How many times have you heard the phrases "over-deliver" and "add value"?

It's easy to promise great value and to mention that your product will over-deliver, and in truth it isn't hard to accomplish. However, it does take effort, energy, and planning. Above all else it simply takes you caring about the results of others. Do that, and achieving success will come easily.

In the webinar example, early on I promised a lot: real methods I was using (along with many successful students) that would allow anyone to move forward and make money with Kindle without having to write—certainly a tall order. I also promised real examples of moneymaking books, how I was able to drive more traffic with less effort than most authors, and more.

This particular webinar and the product itself are focused on six steps I use when creating books to publish to Amazon Kindle. This reduces "information overload" and allows folks to focus on and prioritize the most important elements of publishing books to Kindle that make money. As I walked the audience through the six steps and provided real examples, as well as details on how each step impacts sales and how to ensure success, many attendees' confidence grew in the six steps as well as in me. I over-delivered as promised and the result was lots of sales at a fairly high price: 450-plus sales at $497.

This is a great example of focusing on the golden rule—find out what people want, and give it to them. This rule applies to everything that impacts your online marketing, including how you build your website, what kind of content you publish, keyword phrases you target, videos or podcasts you create, and, of course, the products you develop, all of which will be covered as we move forward.

DEMOGRAPHICS AND THE GOLDEN RULE

Now that you know the importance of figuring out what the market wants and that you need to give it to them, I want to address another important element regarding sales: demographics or market size.

A story comes to mind of when I began to work with Internet marketer Aidan Booth on what would become a joint product between the two of us, Rank and Pillage.

At the time, Aidan had gone through a few of my courses with great success, earning money within weeks of accessing the course materials. Aidan was an amazing student, and I spotted right away that he had a spark and would become very successful in a short time.

Aidan progressed and his results came fast. He studied and, most important, took massive action. After several years he came to me and said he wanted to create his own course on Internet marketing.

We set up a consult and Aidan shared his desires to get started in the Internet marketing niche. We spoke about the types of products he could create. I remember him saying he could not teach SEO or affiliate marketing because I and many others had already covered the topic so well.

This was and is completely false. I mean, can you imagine if only one restaurant sold pizza? And what if there was only one ice cream shop in each major city! I told Aidan that he could easily cover these popular topics by simply including his own special tactics. I also mentioned market size and demographics, and that's what I want to cover right now. One of Aidan's core focuses at the time (and still to this day) was outsourcing, and he mentioned that he could create an entire course around outsourcing that would not impede on my SEO and/or affiliate marketing turf.

While it was true that he certainly could have created such a course, the goal was to impact as many people as possible with this product, and the size of the market that was interested in learning about outsourcing was much, much smaller than folks interested in "making money online."

After all, most people who are interested in outsourcing already have a moneymaking method working for them; they simply want to unload some of the heavy lifting. Again, however, that market is much smaller.

Thus, instead of focusing on a smaller audience that would be interested in outsourcing, we focused the effort toward the much larger "make money" demographic. How can you identify the size of a market prior to investing time and energy creating a product or launching an affiliate site? This will be covered in the upcoming chapter on niche selection. For now, just understand that choosing the right market is incredibly important.

BE IN CONTROL, HAVE A WELL-THOUGHT-OUT PLAN

When it comes to achieving success in anything important in life, it's critical that you have a crystal-clear vision as to exactly what you want. It saddens me that most people have no clear path or plan of action and thus never really understand where they're trying to get to. Of course, if you don't have a clear plan of action, ultimately you'll never reach the destination.

Let's dig deeper. Let's say that someone named Bob became interested in earning money from the comfort of his home. He started researching various moneymaking opportunities online and was fascinated by the different methods he discovered.

He signed up to newsletters from various gurus, attended fascinating webinars filled with amazing success stories, purchased products from different marketers, and ultimately bounced from one opportunity to another.

This story always ends the same, and it happens over and over again in Internet marketing. Bob struggles to achieve life-changing results due to not having a solid plan of action.

He drifts through life, from one project to another, never finishing anything. He does not focus or prioritize his actions to get what he wants, and so he fails.

It's sad. Let's rewrite this story and give it a happy ending!

Bob becomes interested in earning money from the comfort of his own home and starts researching various opportunities that will allow him to do just that.

He is fascinated by the different strategies that so many innovative marketers are using to generate income online.

To achieve meaningful success, Bob understands that he will have to come up with a plan of action and have a vision to reach his desired goals. His first goal is to become educated on the different moneymaking opportunities that are available to him.

Bob studies and learns the basic understanding and how-to knowledge of SEO, video marketing, blogging, podcasting, affiliate marketing, social media marketing, and various other traffic and conversion strategies.

He then looks at his own strengths and weaknesses and creates a plan of action that will allow him to drive traffic and make money.

He looks deeply into his own strengths and weaknesses and decides that video marketing and leveraging YouTube makes the most sense. Bob has always enjoyed amateur photography and videography and decided to combine that love with another—health, fitness and weight loss. Bob's plan is to create a YouTube channel and series of videos on the topic at hand. Some of the videos Bob plans to create will promote nothing, but will simply build trust and add value for those that find his videos. Other videos will in fact promote products and services via various affiliate programs where Bob will have a chance to share his knowledge and expertise and make money.

Perfecto!

Bob is now in control, takes actions based on his overall plan and in a short time begins to get tremendous results online.

I want to reiterate just how important this is: Being in control and knowing what tomorrow and next week will bring and what you will be doing to achieve your desired goal is absolutely paramount to your success.

In November 2009 I planned out my entire year: what I would focus on, how I would spend my time, and ultimately what I would publish and how. In the spring I would launch a product called Auto Content Cash, and later in the summer I would launch my first coaching program focused on Halloween niche marketing.

Once the plan is in place, there is no need to try to figure out what to do or how to spend your time. Focus becomes much easier because now you know what needs to be done to achieve the said goal. Emails from other marketers promoting various products and services take a backseat to your master plan—that plan that allows you to create assets.

PUBLISHING ASSETS

All highly successful marketers create assets online. The process does not have to be complex, hard, or overly time-consuming; rather you simply need to create something that is useful and/or valuable. That's it. Thus, anytime you publish to the Web, ask yourself (and be honest): "Will this be useful or add value?"

That's it. So darn easy!

It doesn't matter whether you're publishing and selling a coaching program for thousands of dollars or uploading a video to YouTube. If what you publish is not useful or adding value for people, you will struggle to get the results you're after, end of story.

Again, let's dig deeper. The most important element of achieving success online is the ability to drive traffic. Being able to achieve a high rank in Google for keyword phrases is considered to be the holy grail of passive, free traffic.

What exactly does targeting a keyword phrase in Google mean?

It's really pretty simple, and I will cover it in more detail in the coming pages. However, for now, understand it's the process of selecting a keyword phrase that people are actually searching for in Google and optimizing a piece of content to rank for that given phrase. In the past, I've referenced the process of creating affiliate sites around Halloween. Thus, I targeted costume search terms such as:

- ghost Halloween kids costume

I then ranked for that very phrase in the Google search engine and featured "ghost Halloween kids costume" on the various pages of the site and linked to various stores with an affiliate link and cashed in, big time!

In 2008, Google unveiled what it called universal search results. Previously, if you had searched Google, you would only find Web pages results. If you wanted news, you would need to click on the news link on the Google homepage to be provided with a list of relevant news results. If you were after videos, once again you would have to click the video link to be presented with video results.

But once Google rolled out universal search, all the search results, including videos, blog posts, news, and more, were combined together. This presented a great opportunity for anyone wanting to rank on page one of Google, for YouTube videos immediately shot to the top of Google for a tremendous amount of keyword phrases.

And since anybody can create a free YouTube account and upload a video, it's really quite easy to rank on page one by leveraging videos on YouTube. However, many marketers were (and are) simply not willing to put themselves in front of the camera to create a video.

Around the same time, several video creation sites sprang up, allowing anyone to easily create a video by stringing together clip art, photographs, or animated characters. The result was lots of low-quality videos being created with the hopes of easy rankings that would lead to an affiliate commission, email signup, or other action.

Here's the rub: The majority of these videos offered no value and were simply not useful to the end user, so while they may have ranked in Google, the desired goal of generating a sale, newsletter signup, or other action was not achieved because the video did not provide value to the end user.

Thus, as you move forward, it is imperative that you create something that will ultimately help people and add value to the Web. When your content is useful, it's a true asset that will have a profound effect on your ability to get results.

As we continue, I'll share how to create asset-based content that is liked, trusted, and leads to sales and conversions. For now, let's move on to another point that can be a make-or-break factor in your journey to online success.

DEALING WITH NAYSAYERS

The number of people who told me no, you can't do it, you shouldn't do it, or doing it would be stupid is beyond ridiculous. Funny thing, these comments almost always came from people who hadn't done it themselves. In fact, as I write this I'm reminded of my very first meetup or "mastermind" with other Internet marketers.

The story begins in Orlando, Florida, in 2008—the year I entered into a new phase of my Internet marketing career by sharing my ideas and strategies about search engine optimization, AdSense, and affiliate marketing. Yes, I had set my sights on becoming a Goo Roo (aka guru)!

At that time, I became affiliated with a small group of peers whom I met through online forums and programs to which I purchased access. We spent hours discussing Internet marketing tactics, and when one of the participants invited me to an exclusive "mastermind" conference scheduled to take place in Orlando, I accepted the invitation with a great deal of excitement.

I purchased my flight to Orlando, booked a hotel room, and packed my bags, eager to meet up and brainstorm with people who spoke my language—Internet marketing geek speak. We all got together for dinner the first night, and when I attempted to say something about marketing, I was asked to "hold off until tomorrow."

Finally, the big day arrived. I grabbed my tinfoil hat and prepared to enter the "secret lab." I was ushered into a hotel room, sat down, and five of the other participants told me they were kicking me out of the group.

What? I had just arrived! Outlandish! Outrageous!

The apparent ringleader laid down the law, and they all agreed that under no circumstances would I be allowed to stay. I later found out that when this guy realized I had set my sights on becoming an Internet marketing guru, he and his followers decided that I wouldn't fit in. He even told me that the strategies he was planning to share were so powerful he could not risk them leaking out beyond the confines of the group. And, of course, since I was planning to teach others Internet marketing, I might allow this highly secretive information to slip out and in the process jeopardize the group's ability to attain optimal results.

So there I was, pleading to stay in the group, but none of them would have it and I was forced to go. The fine chap who invited me in the first place was gracious enough to offer me a ride back to the airport. In all honesty, I was astounded that this so-called friend didn't stand up to the ringleader on my behalf.

Now here's where the story really gets good. You see, the ringleader told me that I would not make it as an Internet marketer because it was much too hard, and he advised me to quit immediately.

"You are wrong," I told him. "I already set my sights, and there is no stopping me now. And I will in fact teach others to become successful Internet marketers as well." I was determined to achieve online success. I wasn't interested in stealing his marketing strategies because I had tons of my own that I had developed during my previous five years as a full-time Internet marketer.

I was ushered out of the meeting room, and the door shut firmly behind me. I headed back to my hotel room, ordered two glasses of wine and some hors d'oeuvres, and had myself a nice man-cry.

I flew back home to Minnesota and got busy. Within a few weeks I launched my second Internet marketing product and sold over five hundred units. I was proud of my accomplishment and excited about the journey I was taking.

Six months later I launched Commission Ritual (copywritten by the amazing Kevin Rogers). That product grossed more than $500,000 in revenue and made me a boatload of money. It put me on the map, giving me a recognized name, and advanced my Internet marketing career to new heights. Most important, it helped *hundreds, if not thousands of marketers* to earn *their first dollars* online. My product added value and for that I am so grateful I did not quit!

Since that first epic failure of an event, I've spoken in Orlando numerous times. The first time I went back, in 2010, I stood in front of just over 100 people, giving a presentation on search engine optimization, driving traffic, and living the dream. The crowd loved it. People were amazed that this was my first presentation. My friend Justin Quick said that I was a cross between Bon Jovi and the Mad Hatter.

Today, when I hear "Orlando," I think about the challenge I faced and how I was unwilling to back down and take no for an answer.

Do not let others tell you what is possible. Do not let others dictate what you will accomplish. You are in control of your own destiny. Many in the world will not wish you well as you journey forward.

Moral of the story: Never listen to the naysayers and don't allow others to dictate your future. When you hit a roadblock, find another path, build a bridge or tunnel, but whatever you do—do not quit!

One of the things I've learned on the journey to success is that you're either growing or falling behind. Having naysayers around can really pull you down mentally. People can be very polarized—either a positive or a negative force in your life. I do my best to distance myself from anyone who is pulling me down. This doesn't mean I don't want to have my work critiqued; it's actually the opposite. I strive to improve and hone my skills, but I pick and choose those around me very carefully. Lastly, I hold no ill will toward those who asked me to leave that super secret meeting in Orlando; in fact, I'm glad it happened. It shaped Brian G. Johnson.

FINDING MY SIGNATURE

In the late 2000s I saw a very motivational video on YouTube focused on an athlete or actor, and in the video I heard a line that became my signature that very second. I would attribute the slogan, but I simply don't remember the source. Here's my signature tagline:

*People **DO NOT** fail at Internet marketing, they simply **GIVE UP** before the magic happens.*

Of course, I tweaked the message with "Internet marketing" and that was that. I typed out that message thousands of times in reports, emails, blog posts, and PowerPoint slides and closed many of my presentations with this saying.

This brings several things to mind and chief among them is this:

How Bad Do You Want It?

Delaying gratification can be extremely challenging. After all, to create a plan, prioritize your actions, and follow through day after day to create a true asset, is the path less taken. It's the day-to-day stuff that is so challenging, and it's nearly impossible to see in the moment.

For example, it's October 17, 2013, and I've been working on this book for about a month now. Every single day my focus is to write more, move forward, and take the steps necessary to complete this project. It takes discipline and is often very hard to follow through on. However, I want that success bad, and when I say *success* I'm not just talking about making a bunch of money —I want to have an impact.

I know that each and every day, as I sit down and begin to write, I will make more and more progress. As I pound the keyboard and voice-dictate this on my MacBook Air, I see I just hit over ten thousand written words. And I know that if I stay on this path and continue to make writing this book a priority every day, in due time I will have a physical book to hold in my hand. Furthermore, I know that the book will be another steppingstone for my career as an Internet marketer and could lead to all kinds of cool things that I want, like speaking engagements and the ability to help more folks achieve success, and that motivates me.

But it's certainly not easy, for delaying gratification is a challenge for anybody.

Risk Versus Reward

This is another area I see so many people struggling with. They tell me they're not sure they want to move forward and put in the effort if it's not going to work.

People DO NOT fail at Internet marketing, they simply GIVE UP before the magic happens.

That's usually my response, coupled with: What is the other option? To play video games, to watch TV, to try to find a better opportunity? Chances are I might end the conversation with "the harder I work, the luckier I get," and it's true: Success is based on what you put in.

Let's take a further look at the day-to-day choices you make. It's still October 17, and I'm still writing this book. I want the outcome, and I'm willing to put in the effort to get it. However, right now my brain is trying to trick me, and it keeps telling me it would be a blast to play some video games. And what would the consequences be if I played a video game instead of writing today? Certainly not the end of the world, and I would have a nice dose of instant gratification. My brain would be happy!

This is the easy choice, to play video games or watch a movie or take my dog for a walk or play Guitar Hero or any of the stuff that provides me with instant gratification. However, over time these easy decisions can lead to an unfulfilling life, a life filled with hoping, wishing, and wondering why things didn't work out. Successful people take the hard road; they're willing to do the things in life that are difficult early on, and over time these things become easy and lead to a desired outcome.

I learned about this in an excellent book by Jeff Olson called *The Slight Edge*, and I recommend that you read it. More important, I hope you train yourself to do what it takes day to day to have an outstanding outcome yourself.

Pushing Past the Fear

Fear of the unknown has stopped so many good people from achieving in life.

Time and time again I've pushed past my fear to do things that were uncomfortable in order to achieve my ultimate goal. Not to sound repetitive, but often this is where the magic happens. Perhaps you have experienced this as well. If not, it's time to give it a try.

Having Vision

We often draw comparisons when talking about *having vision* and *having a goal*. But there is a distinct difference. Having a *goal* means understanding what you want to achieve—a desired outcome or result. Having *vision* is an understanding of what the future will look like, how you will spend your time, the things you will do, and the products and/or services you will offer to achieve that goal. Having vision helps you to peer into your future and understand it.

It also sets your mind to work; that is, your mind will help you and draw you to the things that will help you achieve both your vision and your goal. The times in my life in which I achieved the highest level of success, I had a very clear vision of my future and I understood the steps I would take to achieve my end goal. Having vision like this is incredibly powerful, for there is no second-guessing—you know exactly what needs to be done to achieve the end goal and you just do it. This is especially true if you've set a deadline for yourself (product launches are the ultimate deadline).

THE PRODUCTIVITY RITUAL

Earlier I shared the importance of creating assets to drive your business and make money. That's all well and good if you're productive. However, if you're anything like me, this is a very challenging subject. That being said, over the years I have discovered a simple strategy that has allowed me to conquer distraction and be productive.

Before we move on, let me share with you my thoughts on multitasking: I personally believe it's a myth! I work better when I focus on one primary objective at a time. That doesn't mean I can't do various things in a day; I can and do. However, I never have lots of "big projects" happening at the same time. Rather, I always have one primary goal or target, such as my next big product launch or updating or building a website.

And that is my focus until the primary goal is far enough along that it will yield assets soon and/or in the future. Today, the world moves at the speed of light, distraction is all around us, and *producing assets* can be quite challenging. This is especially true for those of us who spend most of our time online.

So how do we create a productivity ritual that produces those all-important assets that will build a foundation on which our business thrives?

Here are some of the things that have helped me to be more productive.

Create a daily routine

Understand that we live in a noisy world with an endless array of distractions, including friends, family, pets, marketers, companies, bills, social media sites, emails, cell phones, TVs, and more, all vying for our attention.

If you're not aware of this danger, and if you don't make a conscious effort to block these distractions during your "productivity hours," you will struggle to achieve the success you're after.

Thus it's imperative to create a daily routine, or ritual, where you focus and prioritize your time and energy toward the most important thing on your to-do list.

Right now as I write this book it's 9:17 in the morning. I can tell you that over the past two and a half months, in these early hours of the day, I have been focused on this activity of writing *Trust Funnel*, my primary goal. In that timeframe I've written over twenty-three thousand words by just focusing a few hours a day, four days a week.

By focusing my efforts on the one thing that matters the most, I have effectively formed a success habit that continues to push me forward and has allowed me to create and publish asset after asset.

Take inventory of your day-to-day life

This is the first step in creating your own productivity ritual. Do you have a nine-to-five job? Do you have responsibilities like taking your kids to soccer games or feeding your pet? Do you work a part-time job?

Learn how to "pattern interrupt" for the win!

The goal is to identify a block of time in which you can focus yourself to the *one thing* that matters most, the *one thing* that can move you forward and help you produce assets (publishing content that adds value).

Chances are quite good that you will have to sacrifice something in your day to make this time a reality. If you work a day job you might have to steal some hours in the evening, maybe from nine to eleven, to spend on your time block. You almost have to be selfish about this time; it's your time to allow yourself to achieve the success you so very much desire.

If you have a significant other, ask him or her not to interrupt you. If friends call, don't answer the phone. If you love social media, stay off it—otherwise you won't be as productive as you could have been. This is all a hard truth for sure, and early on, when you are first establishing your time block, you might find it challenging.

However, over time you will be drawn to your time block. You will be thinking about working on your primary goal, and you'll look forward to spending this time on your goals and dreams.

If you want it bad enough, you will find the time. And again, all we're talking is just a few hours a day, four days a week. Do that, and watch the sparks fly!

I was able to quit my job by leveraging this very tactic that I am sharing with you here. Having a focus on one thing at a time allowed me to quit that job. Now it's your turn.

The mini-break

One of the things I do during my productive time in the morning is to take mini-breaks after I complete forty-five to sixty minutes of focused work. I do something fun for five or ten minutes.

This could be connecting on Facebook, watching a music video and stretching out, taking Otis (my Standard Poodle) out in the yard and tossing a ball, or playing a level in Plants vs. Zombies on my iPad. Think of the mini-break as a reward that is fun and enjoyable while also stimulating your brain with a new task. The key is to give your mind a rest, to have some fun, and then return to work. If your break becomes a 45-minute online gaming session, it's time to reexamine your priorities.

How much do you want it? If you want it bad enough, you'll figure it out. Remember: Focus on and prioritize your efforts around one primary goal until you complete it.

Your "what" and your "why"

What do you want out of life? That is, what kind of online business do you want to operate and run? Understanding *what you want* your business to look like when it's operating at a high level and generating money is paramount to your happiness moving forward.

I've always had a very clear vision of *exactly* what I wanted my life to look like. I've never been interested in being a top dog, making as much money as possible, having tons of employees, or having a fancy office.

Rather, I've always been interested in running an extremely lean operation and having a simple business I can operate from the comfort of my home—one that provides me freedom and the ability to be nimble with the choices I make day to day.

You might have a completely different vision of what you want your business to look like. Understand there are no right or wrong answers here. My business is awesome and is the *right business for me*; you might want something a bit more complex with more moving parts.

Think about *what* you would like as you build your online business and you'll make decisions that help guide you toward that end.

Now, what is your *why*? You can discover this by answering the question: Why do you do the things you do? When I got started online, my why was to achieve financial independence so I would have the freedom I so desired.

This is fairly common; after all, money buys freedom, toys, new homes, and a fulfilling lifestyle. However, once I got that financial freedom, my *why* changed. I found out that I was really good at being a coach, a motivator, and mentor, and that I was able to help lots of folks get results.

Soon this became my new *why*, to help people achieve their dreams and goals, to help them get the results they desire. I learned that when I help other people to achieve their goals and dreams, it moves me closer to achieving mine. Personally, nothing makes me more excited and happy than to see other folks get a big win.

By understanding my *why*, I'm able to tailor the kind of programs and products that I release to ensure that I'm having the biggest impact on the largest group of people possible.

Personally, I would rather sell a coaching program at a higher price to fewer people than a digital download program to the masses. I do this because I found that I'm able to generate exciting results for many more people when I work with a select group of individuals on an ongoing basis.

Always think about your *why*, and you will make better decisions as you move forward.

Mentor or coach: Identify what you want and find someone who has it

Earlier I mentioned how having a plan of action can reduce the allure of new products being released by various marketing gurus. However, please know that I'm not suggesting you should completely avoid or neglect new products, coaching, or mentoring.

In fact, I'm a huge advocate of finding someone who's doing the thing you want to be doing in the near future and copying them. Of course, this doesn't mean copying an individual marketer step by step; it simply means you should pay attention to those who are where you want to be and doing the things you want to do in order to achieve the success you're after.

Fast-track success

Once you've created your plan of action and know exactly what you want to achieve as you move forward with your business, one of the very best ways to fast-track that success is to participate in a true coaching program.

A coaching program can provide a step-by-step system that is easily followed day to day, allowing members to come out the other side for the better. Coaching programs provide not only step-by-step systems but also the accountability needed to move students forward.

This is one of the reasons why I love offering my students these types of coaching programs. The bottom line is they produce very high-level results in a short amount of time.

Of course, it's incredibly important to choose a coach that walks the walk and talks the talk. Anytime you sign up for a coaching program, make sure there are signs of true success—that is, the coach selling the program has success and/or students who have generated successes. This is a clear sign that the program you will undertake is based on "from the trenches" tactics and strategies that work.

Infiltration: the good ol' boys club

People who have what I wanted have influenced me in a very big way and ultimately led to the creation of the marketer I am. Early on when I got started in Internet marketing, I decided to focus on search engine optimization as well as affiliate marketing.

I found people who were very successful in these areas and followed them. In 2002 and 2003, I spent lots of time asking questions and learning at WebmasterWorld.com. When I began selling my own products and services, I needed to improve my ability to sell via sales copy. Thus, when I ran into Alex Goad, I immediately realized he had many of the skills I was after, including writing persuasive emails, sales copy, sales videos, and more.

Furthermore, when I discovered Alex, he was releasing a product that focused on how to sell digital information products—the *very thing I was already focused on*. This is a perfect example of when it really makes sense to buy a product. After all, I was already focused on the very thing the product was about, and the product vendor had much success doing the very thing he was teaching.

Several years later I actually partnered with Alex as well as Jared Croslow. Together we launched a digital product that generated over half a million dollars in a matter of weeks.

How was I able to get Alex to partner with me?

First off, I joined his monthly program and paid him. If you want to get on somebody's radar, pay them and participate. The last part is pretty important: participate. When I signed up with Alex's program, I made sure I was visible on the forum and I offered support to other people.

Anybody can offer support, whether you're just getting started or you're a seasoned vet. In marketing, when you make yourself available to help other people and share ideas, you will get noticed.

This is exactly what I did, and in time, Alex began promoting my products and soon we partnered together. This is working smart and understanding that it's often not what you know but who you know.

I did the same exact thing in the summer of 2013 when I ran into Joel Comm, the highly successful Internet pioneer and *New York Times* bestselling author. I wanted the opportunity to get closer to Joel, so I paid him. Do not expect highly successful marketers to offer their time, attention, and wisdom for free. Their goal, as it should be, is to support the effort of their paying customers. I knew I could learn a lot from Joel. After all, he was doing the things that I wanted to do.

What was supposed to be a two-day event with about a dozen folks turned into a private one-on-one afternoon. *Perfecto.* This is what I really wanted; perhaps it was meant to be.

I sat with Joel and shared with him my goals over the coming fifteen months, which included the release of a new book backed by Morgan James Publishing (this very book you're reading), more speaking engagements, and a chance to work with him in the future.

Note that prior to this meeting I had already done my homework. I had things in place that would allow me to demonstrate what I was capable of. That meeting resulted in a webinar with Joel for his audience, multiple speaking gigs, and a mentor that has had a massive impact on me in many ways.

Yes, it was scary and challenging to move forward without knowing for sure if I would get what I wanted. Yet I knew deep in my heart that if I kept pushing forward, I would succeed. Things did go my way with Joel, and I am grateful for his help over the last year or so.

Once you know your stuff, figure out a way to get with the people you want to work with. Paying is a very simple and easy way that works much time. Of course, you've really got to know your stuff and bring value to the table.

✔ RECAP:

- **Point of Failure**: Most people fail to *publish assets*. If you don't finish, you will not create assets and you will struggle to achieve your dreams and goals.

- **Focus** on the needs and wants of your potential site visitors and future customers. Do this by leveraging the golden rule of Internet marketing: *Find out what people want, and give it to them.*

- **Market Demographics:** Before jumping into a project, ensure that there is a large enough demographic of people who want what you will focus on creating.

- **Set goals and have a vision** of what your operation will look like when you have the success you're after, and **prioritize** your daily efforts by focusing on the most **essential tasks** that will lead to the success you seek to achieve.

- **Add value and over-deliver.** Add more value than your competitors and you will be amazed at the results your able to generate.

- **Avoid naysayers.** Do not expect everyone to share your enthusiasm; you will encounter bumps in the road.

- **Fast-track success** by getting a **mentor** or **coach** who has done what you want to do and/or has already led other students to success. Paying for access is one of the best ways I know to shorten your success journey. You get what you pay for.

In the next chapter, I'll uncover a common theme found in each and every highly successful individual, not just those in the marketing arena, but in life in general. It's all about personal branding and sharing your message with the world.

CHAPTER 3

SECRET SUCCESS INGREDIENTS— YOUR PERSONAL BRAND

Things are about to get real. Clearly we're not in Kansas anymore! After taking the red pill it's wakeup time! Time for a seismic shift and your plan of action that you will leverage to create tremendous results online. This plan is based on strategies that all high-level players have utilized in some way, shape, or form. It's also the path that few people take. For many it's simply a case of not knowing; others pass up these golden opportunities by letting fear rule their lives and the decisions they make.

Fear often leads to excuses such as, "I'm not good enough, smart enough, good-looking enough (again, spoken in your best *Zoolander* voice), I don't have enough time, I don't have anything to offer, I want to be guaranteed results," and so on.

Many of these secret success ingredients are free or very inexpensive and quick and easy to take advantage of—and beyond a shadow of a doubt they will improve your results, especially when they're combined.

SECRET SUCCESS INGREDIENTS THAT WE'LL COVER
1. **Leverage the Power of Multimedia.**
2. **Discover, Nurture and Build Your Personal Brand, Voice and Audience.**
3. **Focus on Their Wants and Needs.**
4. **Be the Hero!**

They've worked for me as well as my coaching students, and now it's your turn—*if you're ready, willing, and courageous enough to take action.*

FACT: Most people who are searching for a way to make money online have yet to take the red pill. They're searching *outside of themselves* for a cure, an answer, an app, a software program, or a coach or mentor that will give them success.

However, the sad fact is success is never found in an inanimate object or through another person. Some may say that it's not their fault; perhaps they don't know any better or they're brand new to Internet marketing. However, I'm going to suggest that it *is* their fault. After all, they haven't taken control of their lives.

I really hate what ifs as well as should haves and could haves. There is nothing anybody can do about their past; however, each of us has the ability to wipe the slate clean and start anew. The process begins with having the *courage to change the things* we can.

SUCCESS LEAVES CLUES
Nearly all high-level, successful Internet marketers enjoy what I like to call rock star status in the Internet marketing community. When they show up at live events, they are immediately recognized. This does not mean they dress in leather pants or show off for the camera or live audience; rather it simply means that they have built a fan base, are well known, people like them or want to be like them, and they're liked and *trusted.*

People feel as if they almost know them, as if they're friends in some way. When I first started attending Internet marketing events myself, this was the case. People rushed up to me and said they felt like they almost knew me. They wanted to be around me.

How could this be?

The answer is simple. I published content to my marketing blog under my *own name*, just as I'll advise you to do as we move forward. I shared life experiences in business including what was working and what wasn't. Most important, I started using *online video* as soon as the technology was simple enough to make it quick and easy.

Around 2007, the flip camcorder hit the scene and made it really easy to film video specifically for the Web, and YouTube made it simple to publish and distribute that video. I can remember reading a review in *PC Magazine* about the flip camcorder and knew immediately that video was now an option I would be able to leverage. This leads us to Secret Strategy #1:

SUCCESS STRATEGY #1: INCORPORATE MULTIMEDIA INTO YOUR MARKETING MESSAGES

Using multimedia in your marketing messages makes it really easy for people to get to know and like you. This later leads to trust and is where the concept of the Trust Funnel begins.

Just as people get to know characters in their favorite TV shows, Internet marketers who leverage multimedia—especially online video—often become liked and trusted. This leads to far easier traffic generation as well as conversions, ultimately making it much easier to make significant money.

Game-changing results are very possible simply by leveraging multimedia including online radio programs (podcasting and/or Internet radio shows) and online videos (content videos uploaded to YouTube, sales videos, lead-capture videos, and more). Another incredibly powerful multimedia format is webinars, which can be used to teach, sell, coach, and mentor.

Multimedia is the secret ingredient that's been hiding in plain sight for so many. It's the thing that few focus on; in fact, many avoid it all together. No wonder they struggle!

Furthermore, the success that can be gained by leveraging these publishing platforms is driven by old-school marketing fundamentals such as storytelling, speaking, and presenting to an audience (both on video and in person).

These fundamentals that I speak of are not sexy, require a bit of thought and effort, and cannot be leveraged at the push of a software button. They require focusing on one's self and skills that need to be learned and developed over time.

Unfortunately this is not something that most are willing to do. Rather, they continue to look for the solution outside of themselves as I mentioned earlier.

For these reasons, few of the marketing products that are released target these skills. Heck, look at my golden rule:

Find out what people want, and give it to them.

Instead, most of the products that hit the market today are focused on a tactic or method that promises quick results, more traffic, or social engagement—and ultimately quick and easy profits. Even worse, some of these products claim results that can be generated without the need to write content, put yourself on video, or generally do anything that adds value for the end user.

This is the proverbial rabbit hole, and it runs incredibly deep. Often buyers of these products end up publishing subpar content that doesn't build trust or add value. And when it comes to Web marketing, you're either adding value or you're annoying people. What do you do when you find low-quality content?

Whether it's a video, blog post, or podcast, if you're like 99 percent of online surfers, you leave never thinking twice. Subpar content produces subpar results, plain and simple.

This doesn't mean you need to release a *perfect* product. Rather, you need to add value and care. Do these two things and you will impact people. Do this over and over and you will build a following—and be on your way to achieving your dreams and goals.

For the record, there's nothing wrong with a product offer that focuses on a method or tactic. Heck, I've released several of these types of products myself, and they can be incredibly effective.

What's important to understand is that it's *all of these elements* that lead to success—the best plugins, social media, and search tactics, as well as putting yourself out there, leveraging multimedia, adding real value with the content you publish, and building up trust. Leave out personality, and grabbing attention becomes much more difficult!

Take inventory right now of all the top Internet marketers you know. Do they do these things? Do they focus on the latest strategies and tactics to build traffic?

For some the answer is yes, but not for all of the top-level players.

Do they leverage social media?

Most do, but not all.

But what's the thing they all focus on, time and time again?

The answer is Success Strategy #2? Here it comes ...

SUCCESS STRATEGY #2:
BUILD YOUR BRAND, YOUR VOICE, AND YOUR AUDIENCE

What exactly does that mean? Successful marketers know that their brand is *who they are*—the whole package. When it comes to their voice, it's how they speak, the language and vocabulary they use day to day, on camera, in webinars, and onstage.

It's their style, or lack thereof, with the clothes they wear and the way they carry themselves. It's the gestures they use. It's how they act day to day, and the key ingredient is *authenticity.*

The goal is to become the very best you possible. Never try to be someone else. This often happens, and the results are always terrible.

Rather, strive to become the very best YOU possible and embrace all that you are. In time you will find and grow your voice and audience.

Here's another secret for you: When you do these things—when you put yourself out there—everything becomes easier. Traffic flows, visitors like and return to your site for your content, you rank higher in Google, people sign up to your list, and they buy your products as well as other people's products that you endorse and recommend.

Sounds scary!

This is the crux of the matter, uploading a video in which you're speaking in front of the camera, presenting onstage to a live audience, recording an audio program such as a podcast, or maybe just launching a blog under your own name. It seems really scary for so many, and it requires stepping outside of your comfort zone—the very place that the magic happens.

For these reasons, lots of people just don't. Instead they continue looking for that *one thing* or *person* outside themselves that will give them the results they're after, and the cycle continues.

Down the rabbit hole they go ...

This could have easily been the case for me. Honestly, putting yourself out there is scary. However, I wanted success bad enough that I have been willing to do whatever it takes to get it. So I moved forward and faced my fears. I failed often, and it was a bumpy journey, however I pressed on.

Brian G. Johnson Version 1.0

When I first set out to create my own personal "Brian G. Johnson" brand, I dressed like, sounded like, and acted like so many who were already in the Internet marketing space. I can remember recording the very first video I uploaded to YouTube. I read from a script, with little personality, and was BOOORING! However, I did it, and little by little over the next few years my authentic self began to push out, and people responded.

🐾. Pro Blogging, Make Money Adsense - My-Affiliate-Progra…

What's interesting is that even when I was just getting started and clearly was not that great on camera, people still responded very favorably. Within a few weeks I had published a handful of videos, and the response was tremendous.

I was sharing my own experience-based solution, and I was real—and that is what people want. Over time I got better, as did my results.

You can duplicate what I've done simply by getting started. You don't have to be perfect or share the most amazing thing ever. You just have to get started and focus on the wants and needs of your future audience.

No excuses.

Fast forward to 2014, and you'll find Brian G. Johnson Version 3.0. I have continued to seek out how to be a better marketer, and I have put what I've learned into play in a number of ways, including sharing my silly personality and sharing new strategies and tactics based in social media, Kindle, and more.

Yes, it took guts to begin sharing my goofy side, but in time it got easier and easier. Also note that today, the new and improved "authentic" and slightly crazy Brian tends to get more positive feedback and certainly grabs attention with more people.

I'm not saying you should act goofy like me. What I am saying is that the more you share your authentic self, the better. It's all about finding your voice and sharing it. We'll talk more about finding your voice in just a bit.

What I learned was that many of my fears were unwarranted and downright silly. The more often I faced them and did the things that scared me, the easier they became. A great example of this is the videos I published to YouTube.

I still get nervous prior to presenting from the stage. However, I also know that I get tremendous feedback each and every time I do speak, and it gets easier and easier with practice.

SUCCESS STRATEGY #3:
GIVE YOUR END USERS WHAT THEY WANT

Remember, it's not about you. It's about your visitors, subscribers, and buyers.

You may think you simply don't have anything to offer, that you're not attractive enough and can't produce video and audio files that anyone would want to listen to or watch; or you may think that anything you could offer has already been published by other marketers.

However, none of these items is the focus of what *the end user really wants,* and for this reason anyone willing to move forward and take action can leverage these strategies to generate game-changing results.

Here's why: This type of thinking is focused on *you* the publisher rather than the *end user,* and what matters to them is whether you can help them with the problem they're facing. They're not interested in how pretty or handsome you are. They will be incredibly forgiving on the technical details, such as lighting or audio, as long as what you publish is good enough and provides insight into their problem.

It's not about you, it's about them. I suggest you get over it!

Remember, people want *authenticity, real solutions,* and *life experiences,* which by the way can be either good and/or bad.

Even if you're just getting started in the topic you've chosen, you can move forward and publish under your own name and offer content that matters to people—content that will instill trust and push you to where you want to go.

IT'S ALL HOW YOU FRAME IT

Earlier I mentioned playing your hand to the best of your ability, and this is a great example for us to explore. Let's say you're interested in getting started in the photography niche. This is a niche market you've identified as potentially lucrative, and you've also got a lot of passion about learning digital photography.

Now, if you're truly passionate about the subject of photography, you'll be learning a lot about the given subject. Chances are you'll be reading, researching, and testing various new ways to take digital pictures with cameras, camcorders, as well as your smartphone. You will also likely be experimenting with various software programs and apps that will help you get the most out of the pictures you take.

This is exactly the kind of thing that so many people online would be interested to learn, and you now have a tremendous opportunity to share the lessons you've mastered and help people to move forward with digital photography while making money at the same time. Wow!

But, you say, *I'm not an expert. People want to hear from experts!*

Well, this is true. People *do* want to hear from experts, and often they also want to hear from people who are *passionate* about their favorite subject. This is where you and I both have a chance to play what I like to call "the newbie" card.

If I were to launch a website covering digital photography, and I was fairly new to the subject, this is what I would include:

Hello, and welcome to Digital Photography World!

My name is Brian G. Johnson. I'm fairly new to digital photography but incredibly passionate and enthusiastic about capturing special moments as they happen. I launched this website to share my experiences as I explore the latest techniques, trends, and hardware in the digital photography space. Already, I've learned some amazing techniques that you can find right here on my site.

Subscribe to my newsletter now and never miss a future update!

DAY-ONE EXPERTS

Allow me to share something very powerful that I learned from Alex Goad. There is a wide-open opportunity for anybody—and I mean anybody—who wants to jump in and build a following online, and no previous experience is needed!

Sound impossible? Does that sound like a scam?

Well, let's dive deeper and take a look. One of the things people are interested in when researching, studying, and gathering information on a favorite hobby or niche market is tools of the trade. And this is where we all have a massive opportunity to grab the spotlight, drive lots of traffic, build a list, and of course, make money.

As for tools of the trade, every niche market has them, whether we're talking digital photography, health and fitness, weight loss, the foreign currency exchange market (FOREX), search engine optimization, building a website, gardening, or whatever.

All of these niche markets are about learning a new set of skills. They're "how-to" markets, and many of these how-to skills are focused on the usage of products and services. This is where opportunity shines bright for those just getting started.

When new products are released to the market, people interested in those niche markets are going to want to know about those very products: Are they helpful? Are they worth it? What's the best way to use them? What are the advantages of using these new products and/or services?

There's zero information published about these products because, well, they're brand new and nobody has used them up until the release date. Thus, anybody with a little bit of go-get-'em attitude can review these products, educate the market, and also drive traffic and even generate an affiliate commission (we'll cover how to do this in the coming pages).

Consider the social marketing site Pinterest for example. Prior to the closed beta (March 2010), there were no Pinterest marketing experts; there couldn't be as the site was just launching.

However, during the summer of 2010, the site grew to more than ten thousand users, and many people started sharing ideas about how to use and leverage the site to drive traffic. These early adapters were in fact the leading experts when it came to Pinterest. New products and services offer a tremendous opportunity.

Just head to YouTube and search for "unboxing," and you will find thousands and thousands of videos of people unwrapping brand-new tech products and reviewing them.

New products and services also offer a great opportunity to drive easy traffic as they are what I like to call *just-born keywords*. After all, nobody knew that the latest version of the iPad would be called the iPad Air. Thus, early adapters who targeted the iPad Air for review had a much easier time ranking for the phrase than someone targeting "iPad tutorial."

Let's take yet another example, something outside of the tech industry. Let's look at the gardening niche. While writing this book, I went to Google and searched for "new gardening products 2013."

This search led me to: *the Flexi Spray ...*

The Flexi Spray is a new hose and spray head that can be wrapped around a tree or stake, allowing users to water a specific area.

I also went to Google and searched for Flexi Spray and noticed a number of searches that Google recommended, one of which was "Flexi Spray review."

And, surprise, surprise, there was a YouTube video of a man showing how to use this new Flexi Spray that was released in 2013. This particular video ranked number two in Google and is driving considerable traffic.

This strategy requires no black hat tactics or trickery, no complex software or marketing shenanigans, and it can be leveraged in nearly all big-money niche markets.

Anybody can be an expert; it's just a matter of playing the hand you've been dealt. If you're new to a niche market, you play the "rookie of the year" card. If you have years and years of experience with the niche market, that's the card in your hand to play. It's all about perspective and spin.

GETTING STARTED ON A SHOESTRING BUDGET

When getting started it is not necessary to spend thousands of dollars on hardware and software. You also don't need to be a tech genius to publish content that gets results.

Having a beautiful, cutting edge, and professional website is an asset. However, it's not nearly as important as the content the site offers. Users in search of a remedy or solution would much rather find value-added content that addresses their needs and wants rather than a pretty site with average content that does not offer them a solution.

When it comes to online video, again, people would much, much rather find a video that offers true step-by-step advice to help them solve their problem than a whiz-bang video filled with effects but not much substance.

Publishing content that not only looks fantastic but offers users what they're truly looking for has never been less expensive. In fact, chances are good that you already possess much of what's needed for you to move forward and publish content that can and will drive results.

If you own an iPhone or similar smartphone you already possess a fantastic video camera that fits in your pocket. I've personally filmed many online videos that look great and sound fantastic with my iPhone 4S (the model released in 2011).

If you own a tablet or iPad, there are many apps you can download to create powerful video presentations that again will address the wants and needs of your viewers and also get results. Over the last few years I've used an app called Doodlecast—which costs a whopping $2.99 to record videos— that has generated five-figure commissions for me. As we dive deeper into content creation, I'll share the software and hardware products I use to "crush it" online. You simply don't need to spend a fortune to get results today.

FINDING YOUR VOICE

When it comes to success, non-authenticity stands out like a sore thumb. Whether you look for examples in sports, entertainment, or business, the most successful people are always incredibly authentic.

Variety is the spice of life, right?

What's the best flavor of ice cream: chocolate, strawberry, or vanilla? Ice cream giant Baskin-Robbins knew that by offering thirty-one flavors they would appeal to more people and thus capture more business.

And when people are looking to learn a new skill or gain knowledge in a chosen field, they gravitate toward people they know, like, and trust.

By sharing your passion—and your own authentic "flavor"—with the world in the content you publish, whether that be a video you upload to YouTube or an article you post to your blog, you'll connect with your audience, which is comprised of those that share similar traits and passions.

If you love numbers, for example, or you're big on science, then by sharing your excitement for these subjects you will draw people to you that also share a love for all things numeric and/or scientific.

Or perhaps you're a ham and enjoy making people laugh. By being true to who you are, you can draw other goofballs into your Trust Funnel, have a boatload of fun, and make life-changing income all at the same time.

And here's the kicker …

It's so much easier to embrace who you are with others when you're not trying to be something that you're not. This is the essence of having a voice and being authentic, and it's something that comes over time. Just as we evolve as we move through life, so will your marketing voice. Take your business seriously, strive to add value with the content you publish, but understand that this does not mean you have to take *yourself* seriously.

The core of the Trust Funnel you will build as we move forward is your voice and your brand—an incredibly powerful marketing tool that only you can leverage. Lots of marketers make the mistake of trying to appeal to everyone with the goal of driving more sales. However, by trying to appeal to everyone, you in fact appeal to no one and end up alienating your true audience.

SUCCESS STRATEGY #4: BE THE HERO!

So many people today are bored to death. They spend most of their waking hours somewhere they'd rather not be, often with those they have no real connection with. They find themselves working a nine-to-five as a matter of necessity; thus, they cherish weekends, holidays, and time spent with friends and family. People are looking for a chance to escape from their dull day-to-day lives.

This is why guys love gangster movies and summertime blockbusters that feature lots of explosions and whiz-bang effects. It's the same reason why women love shoe shopping: It provides a break from the daily grind.

This offers a tremendous opportunity to grab attention by playing into the whole "rock star status" thing I mentioned earlier. It also provides you a chance to stand out from the crowd by sharing your personality as well as the hero that lives within you (there's one in all of us).

In 2013 I released a coaching program called Revenge of the Affiliates. I had a clear idea of the imagery I would use on the sales page. I wanted exciting—that is, a cross between James Bond and *Star Wars*, stuff blowing up and action!

While we're exploring the subject of bringing out your inner hero, let's take a look at some famous personalities who've done that with killer results.

Do you know Matthew Lesko?

If you answered no, you're not alone. Most people don't know Matthew by name; however, mention the crazy guy on TV that wears suits with large question marks all over them and heads begin to nod.

Lesko has written a number of books on federal grant money and how everyday folks can get access grants as well as products and services that can change their lives. This is a very competitive niche market for sure, and Lesko often appears on late-night infomercials by being slightly kooky and interesting. Lesko carved out his spot, his brand and his voice.

According to Wikipedia, Bill Nye is:

An American science educator, comedian, and television host. Stop and think about that for a minute.

- Science educator
- Comedian
- Television host

Nye has grabbed the attention of millions of people by using *comedy* and *creating excitement* for kids and adults alike in the world of science. He's widely known as a science expert, but he's also a kooky guy who makes learning science *fun*.

Like Bill Nye, you can become the hero that so many are after, whether they know it or not. You can provide the break from the day-to-day grind for your audience, giving them something to believe in, something to cheer about—the hero they're looking for.

YOUR SUPERHERO STORYLINE

During 2013 and 2014, I studied a lot of sales copy from some very smart and persuasive copywriters, including Perry Belcher and Colin Theriot. During this time one common theme emerged and that was developing a superhero storyline.

Colin wrote an article on this very topic, and at the top of the post there was an illustration from a comic book. Later I heard Perry present his twenty-one step sales sequence and the importance of developing a storyline. He mentioned that storylines from comic books are great examples of how to craft your own "superhero" storyline.

By incorporating a superhero into your marketing storyline, you address a glaring issue that prevents people from taking action and purchasing, and that is believability. It's a huge struggle for many people to believe they can achieve high-level results.

However, by offering people a product that features a system or formula as well as a superhero, the pressure is no longer on them to produce results but rather is dependent on the formula and/or superhero.

HERO ELEMENTS TO INCLUDE IN YOUR STORYLINE

Backstory, Early Days

How did you get to where you are now? When composing your personal storyline, remember to play the hand you've been dealt! If you've just gotten started, then play the rookie hand. If you've been at it for a long time, play the veteran hand.

Incorporate the good, the bad, and the ugly—it makes you authentic and relatable to your audience (and those who may become your future audience). If you've had some struggles to get where you are now, by all means share that. If you made some mistakes along the way, congratulations, you're human!

Furthermore, by sharing struggles and mistakes, you can help others to bypass pitfalls they may experience along the way.

Make Them Laugh

People love to laugh. Heck, laughing is a sign of having fun, so if you can make someone laugh and still get your point across, you've got gold. This was a lesson that took me a while to learn. People often remark that I'm a pretty fun guy to be around, and that's true. I'm also a great teacher and coach, educator and entertainer.

If you look at the A-level players in the Internet marketing "guru" space, humor is an attribute that is often present. However, this doesn't mean you have to be funny. Focus on being engaging and memorable, one way or another.

Accomplishments

Why should people listen to you? What can you do for them! It's about their journey, not yours. By highlighting your accomplishments, you're ultimately pointing out stuff they very well may like to achieve. Do that, and people will listen to you.

In 2010 I launched a $500 coaching program and earned six figures in a matter of days. Lots of Internet marketers would like to do just that, so when I tell that story and they hear what I've accomplished, I've got their ear. They may think, *Wow, I want to do that one day.*

Flaws

Just as you should include your failed attempts, mistakes, and struggles, you should also share your flaws. I'm certainly flawed—my grammar and spelling are horrid, I've struggled with confidence issues, and I'm great at sticking my foot in my mouth by saying the wrong things and lots more. Once again, sharing your flaws makes you more human and easily approachable.

Your Moral Code

What principles do you stand by? Do you have a moral code that you live by? These principles should be woven into the stories you tell. Doing so will impact people. As you craft your storyline, consider:

- What don't you like?
- What gets under your skin?
- What really fires you up?

Make sure to let your audience know, especially when those principles are based in the niche market you're in.

Language, Phrases ...

Do you have a favorite saying that few other people use? If so, make sure to incorporate that into the content you publish and the stories you tell. This includes buzzwords as well as the phrases and even *how* you talk. If you're from the South and have a slow Southern drawl, then embrace that. Perhaps you're from the Bronx and you speak fast—really fast!

Then announce it! "Hey, I'm from New York. I speak fast and this is some important stuff about blah, blah, blah ... so listen up!"

Remember, the key is that you're after the one thing that people rarely give up—their attention—so use your own unique personality to get it!

Also, if you're just getting started in a particular niche market, make sure to identify how people (ultimately your prospects) in that niche already talk and the buzzwords they use. For example, gamers have a very colorful vocabulary. They don't *beat* an opponent, they *own* them. When a game is getting really exciting and fun, they may shout out, "WOOT! WOOT!"

If you want to sell to folks, make sure you're using their vocabulary, and they will more readily listen to you.

Go Weird

Are you a little bit eccentric? Do your friends think you're a bit off? If so, congratulations, because you can use that to gain—yep—attention! Dance to the beat of your own drum, fly that freak flag, and let people make comments about you. After all, you want them to be talking about YOU rather than someone else.

Likeable

Above all, be likeable because:

"People listen to those they like and buy from those they trust."

Be weird, colorful, flawed, and funny, but don't be so weird that people don't like you. The goal is to be yourself, have fun, and be engaging. And always, always lead with what your audience wants!

Approachable

Be approachable. If you show up at an event or are recognized, others should be fairly comfortable with the idea of introducing themselves to you.

Priorities!

All of these characteristics should be incorporated into your storyline and shared in the content you publish. Whether it's a sales video, blog post, or Facebook update, these items should be included from time to time. But remember they aren't the core focal point.

Again, it's not about you but rather what you can do for your subscribers or browsers. Whatever niche you've decided on, *that is the priority and focal point* for all the content you publish. But you can certainly add color and grab attention by leveraging your unique style and voice when delivering your message to your audience.

Turn to the golden rule: *Find out what people want, and give it to them.*

PERCEIVED VALUE

Perception is a very interesting thing online, and over the years I have found that people's *perception of value* as well as *expert status* is highly influenced by a number of factors that you can control and leverage to your benefit.

Visual appearance is one such element, and it's incredibly easy to take advantage of this factor when creating a website, product, or offer. The time and money spent on making any Web property look professional is rather insignificant when considering the benefits.

There are a number of ways to ensure your site and product offers look awesome. You can pay someone to do the work for you, you can use free and paid WordPress themes (for site visuals), and you can also use a number of tools online to create great product box shots.

For example, MarketingEasyStreet.com is my marketing blog, and I'm able to leverage it to build my list, sell products as an affiliate, and more. I've done this by following the exact blueprint I'm sharing with you in this book.

Currently, the site is running on the OptimizePress 2 WordPress theme. This theme offers a ton of power and looks fantastic but also comes with a bit of a learning curve. We'll talk more about theme selection as we move forward. I also hired a graphics designer to create logos, headers, and other visuals for a modern, professional-looking website.

VISUAL WIZARDRY

Another excellent way to increase the perceived value of a product you're offering is to include a product shot on your website. Whether it's a free offer in exchange for an email address (list building) or a product you're selling, an image of the product can only boost conversions (as long as the image looks professional), and the cost is rather insignificant.

You have several options when it comes to product box shots. You can pay a designer to create all the images needed for a project, including headers, footers and logos for your website. Or you can use a Web-based service to create product images—many of which are quite inexpensive.

✔ RECAP:

- **Success Comes From Within:** Success is not found or purchased via a marketing product; rather it comes from within. Find and leverage **your personal brand and voice.** This will lead to you becoming "Internet famous," and your audience will begin to know, like, and trust you.
- **Technology Fast Track:** Use online video and other forms of multimedia to connect with others quicker and ultimately build your trust.
- **Do Not Live in Fear:** Speaking, creating videos, and sharing yourself online can be scary for sure. However, people don't care about what you look or sound like. They care about what you can do for them. Focus on and prioritize the problems your potential site visitors, subscribers, and future buyers have, and provide solutions for them.
- **Day-One Experts:** Leverage new products, opportunities, and ideas, and soon people will see you as an expert.
- **Success Secret Ingredients:**
- **Be the hero**, find **your voice,** and build **your audience**.
- Create a **memorable brand**, increase **perceived value** by using professional **visual elements** including a great-looking site via a WordPress theme, as well as **product images and graphics**.
- Create a **unique selling position** to ensure you're able to communicate what your product offers quickly and easily.

In the next chapter, I will share the mystery that is Google and how trust has become such a big factor in the Google ranking algorithm.

CHAPTER 4

THE EVOLUTION OF GOOGLE RANKINGS AND THE TRUST MATRIX

I n the previous chapter we focused on how you can build and leverage your own personal brand and voice to appeal to future visitors to your website and social properties. In this chapter we'll take a look at the mechanics and evolution of ranking in Google.

Specifically, we're going to take a deep look at how the "big sites" like Google Search, Facebook, Google+, YouTube, and Twitter leverage user engagement or *similar "trust" elements* in their algorithms to determine which content is made more visible.

WILLY WONKA'S CHOCOLATE FACTORY

Like Willy Wonka's chocolate factory, understand that nobody knows *exactly* how the Google algorithm works. Anyone who claims they *fully understand* the "Google Algo" either works at Google or is living in la-la land. Thus, as we move forward, I'm going to share where I believe the future of search rankings are heading. Many of my peers already believe we are there, and that may be the case. I'll also share what I and many SEO experts believe to be helpful strategies when it does come to ranking well in Google.

What I am certain of is this: Leveraging the strategies found in Trust Funnel will have a positive impact on your website and garner a favorable response with humanoids. Ultimately, that is exactly what Google wants to provide to its users—*easy access to webpages that add value and can be trusted.*

LINK BUILDING, WEB SPAM, AND GOOGLE

In the coming pages, I'll share how and why links have become so important when it comes to ranking well in the Google search engine. For this reason, may SEO experts focus on the tasks of "link building," that is, creating links that link to their own site. However, I will not touch on this subject within this book, as I don't believe it will serve your best interests or mine.

Here's why: Back in the day, SEO experts focused on *building links* to attain high search rankings, which in turn led to targeted traffic to one's website.

Often times, link building can have a positive impact on your rankings. And, just as often, the practice of building links to a particular site or webpage can also result in a Google penalty which can reduce traffic to zero.

Today, there are many things you can do to *promote* and *market* your website that will result in the same type of *targeted traffic to your site*, minus the risk. There's a natural correlation between the amount of links a website naturally attracts and traffic that flows to the site.

Furthermore, I personally believe that focusing on content—which can also drive traffic from the big sites—is more fun, more productive, and better serves you and your audience.

It's these big sites that can make or break your business, so understanding how and why they rank content will give you an edge in an ethical manner. We're also going to look at how these sites have *incorporated trust signals from one another* into their ranking algorithm to ultimately form what I like to call a **trust matrix**.

The trust matrix is a massive departure from the algorithm that powered Google years ago. Once the trust matrix is understood, it is far easier to drive more traffic based on the content you publish to the Web.

Tip: Anytime you publish something to the Web, always think of a) appealing to actual visitors that may find your content, and provide value to those visitors, and b)incorporating words they may enter into the Google search engine into the content you're publishing. Doing so will often result in more traffic from Google to your published content, whether that's a blog post, a Kindle book, or a video posted to YouTube.

As we move into the topic of publishing content to your marketing blog, you'll be able to leverage my 12-Step Trust Funnel Ranking Formula located in chapter nine, which will walk you through this exact process.

To better understand how the *trust matrix* impacts the flow of traffic across the Web, let's take a look into the early Google algorithm and how it determined webpage rankings.

ROBOTS AND EVOLUTION OF THE EARLY GOOGLE ALGORITHM

In 1997, two college students named Larry Page and Sergey Brin began collaborating and developed a search engine they called BackRub. They ran their operation on Stanford University servers, and their search engine quickly gained momentum and became quite popular with college students. Soon Larry and Sergey moved their operation off college grounds and servers and renamed their search engine Google. By 1998, Google was hailed by *PC Magazine* for its ability to return highly relevant search results. Not surprisingly, the popularity of Google grew at a feverish pace.

The Google algorithm that determined which webpages ranked well and which did not was based on *how webpages linked to one another*. This was a massive departure from other search engines that were based on content and keyword phrases found on the webpage itself. Thus, search rankings were easy for webmasters to manipulate.

With the Google search engine, rankings were harder to game as they were determined by how *other webpages* linked to a particular webpage. Ultimately, Google had a better, more secure algorithm that delivered better results for its users ... for a while anyway.

POWERED BY ROBOTS: THE ACHILLES HEEL FOR GOOGLE

During this time, Google delivered better results to its users. However, those results were still determined by robots. Google robots crawled the web and collected data that was based on factors that, in time, were easy to exploit. Links played a massive role in which webpages ranked and which ones did not.

Thus, webmasters got really creative in feeding the robots the very thing that increased rankings: links. Webmasters began trading "reciprocal links," established "link farms" to boost rankings, and various software packages became available that built links nearly at the push of a button.

However, as the years passed it became increasingly hard to manipulate their algorithm, and while links have always played a big role, other factors such as trust became increasingly important in establishing high Google rankings.

THE PIVOT: GOOGLE, FACEBOOK, "LIKES," AND HUMANOIDS

This is the pivot and it's also where we dip our toe into the *theory* of the Google search algorithm. Once Google begins to implement social signals into its algorithm, humans will influence the rankings.

Think about that.

Social engagement (likes, shares, and comments found on blogs and social sites like Facebook, Twitter, and Google+) are based on **human activity**. It is not based on something that can be easily exploited, such as a robot.

When was the last time you liked, shared, or commented on content found on a social site that you generally did not like?

If and when Google begins to incorporate social signals from sites such as Facebook, Twitter, Google+, LinkedIn, Instagram, and Pinterest into its algorithm, it will no longer be powered solely by a robot that is easy to exploit.

Today, many SEO experts, including myself, agree that not only is the algorithm powered by robots and a mathematical equation, but it is also influenced by the actual *Web surfers* who are landing on your webpage!

And it's not just social signals that Google could be mining to determine if users actually like your site. If the surfer who landed on your webpage leaves within seconds, that's a clear signal that they did not like the content and thus the webpage they found.

Furthermore, what if Google was able to determine things like:

- How long a visitor spent on your site
- How many pages of your site they visited
- How often a visitor returned to your website

In my humble opinion, this is exactly what was behind the more recent Google updates that may have included the infamous Panda and Penguin updates of 2011.

For the sake of argument, however, let's say I am wrong and human activity does *not* play a role in the Google algorithm. If you adopt this type of thinking you will *win* for you will be creating a site that people like and thus they will share, like, link to, return to, and sign up for your newsletter—all of the things that will contribute to the success you're after.

Ka-BOOM!

Google Panda and Google Penguin have become the "gatekeepers" that prevent low-quality webpages from ranking due to *actual visitors* not liking the webpage in question.

Now you may be wondering, *How in the world is Google able to determine whether visitors to my site, blog, YouTube video, etc., like my content?*

Trust Factors and Google

So, how can Google know? I mean, how can they actually know if people "like and trust" your site? Let's dig deeper and see just how far this rabbit hole goes.

1) Google Chrome

According to W3Schools, today more than 50 percent of Web surfers use Google Chrome as their browser of choice. Think about that! This is a Web browser created by Google that stores data and information on an individual's computer based on how they surf the Internet—which sites they return to often, how much time they spend on those sites, and much more.

Google claims that it does not use the data collected by Chrome, but most SEO experts agree that it would be quite easy to factor this kind of data into the rankings algorithm.

Link to citation: http://www.seoroundtable.com/google-chrome-search-usage-15618.html

2) Google Analytics

Google Analytics is a Web-based application that collects website-user statistics such as:

- How long a user lingers on a particular website
- How many pages a user visits on a particular website

- Percentage of people who leave a site as soon as they land on it (this is known as bounce rate)
- And more …

The above are the telling elements that can easily determine the likability of websites. After all, when visitors land on a site and stay there for thirty minutes to browse through multiple pages, that is a clear indication that they like what they see. On average, most people leave websites within less than one minute.

These factors, by the way, are what most SEO experts would have you focus on—that is, creating a trustworthy and likable website that you will then optimize for multiple page visits where more time can be spent as well as social engagement (comments, likes from Facebook, etc.). How to optimize a website so that people trust and like it will be covered in detail in the coming pages of this book.

This is the *trust matrix at work*—all the big sites working together and leveraging similar data based on *likes, trust,* and *visitor engagement.*

And this leads me right back to: "People listen to those they like and buy from those they trust."

Thus, the goal moving forward will be to add value and be trusted along the way.

A POWERFUL QUESTION

One simple question can ensure you're always moving in the right direction:

Can and will this action be trusted and does it add value?

If you ask yourself this before doing anything online, you will always make decisions that lead you to the success you're after. This can apply to anything you do to enhance your brand: posting a simple article to your site, uploading a video to YouTube, posting a status update to Facebook, launching your first product, or even registering a domain name.

This simple question will always steer you in the right direction.

Each time you publish anything online, ask yourself, "Can and will this action be trusted and does it add value?" Publish high-quality content that adds value, and it will be liked. Furthermore, it will send a clear signal to Google that can and will improve your rankings over time.

It all begins with the understanding that each decision you make regarding what and how you publish has an impact, for better or worse. Stuff you probably never realized can have an impact, such as your domain extension, how long you registered your domain, how long your site has been online, whether Google finds duplicate content on your site, and lots more. I will cover these factors in the coming pages to ensure you make the right moves.

Don't worry about making a mistake; simply refer to the simple question and you will win: *Can and will this action be trusted and does it add value?* This question applies to humans who find your published content and the robots that creep and crawl across the Web.

Of course, not every small decision will make or break your marketing efforts. However, they do add up to paint a very clear picture of *your overall intentions* and the *positive* or *negative* value you add to the Web.

In the next chapter we'll turn our attention to a topic of utmost importance: choosing your niche market, the "space" where you will create your Trust Funnel.

CHAPTER 5

CHOOSING YOUR NICHE MARKET

Y ou may very well already have a niche in mind. Perhaps you want to launch a website to drive traffic to an already established moneymaking business. Or maybe you have an existing website online that you want to focus on.

You can use the strategies and tactics found in this book to do both of these things.

However, if you're just getting started or want to increase your earnings, then we need to talk about the niche market you will enter and how you will make money. Niche selection is incredibly important and will have a massive impact on your results.

Choose the right niche and you can make mistake after mistake and still make piles of money. Choose the wrong niche and making money becomes a difficult proposition, like trying to get blood from a rock.

So how do I find the right niche, you ask?

The process begins by understanding exactly what your end goal will be and that is: to help people get results and/or overcome a problem or issue they're facing. Do this and money will come easily and often.

Getting results and/or overcoming issues may include growing a flower garden, losing weight, finding a boyfriend or girlfriend, learning Photoshop or digital photography, setting up a website or blog, teaching SEO or affiliate marketing, or sharing your personal experience with cooking (the list is almost endless).

As I mentioned earlier, we'll focus on *digital product niche markets* as they offer you a chance to get started as an affiliate (easier) and then later become a vendor for more earning potential.

YOUR TRUST FUNNEL VISION

Before we jump in and discuss how to select a digital niche market, let's take a look at what your *Trust Funnel will look like* when it's operational. This is having vision in business, and by understanding and actually envisioning the operation of your Trust Funnel you will be able to make better decisions moving forward. Furthermore, this process will engage the creative powers of your subconscious mind.

PUBLISH ACROSS THE BIG SITES

The end goal is to establish an *asset* that is your marketing blog. You'll have created an asset once the site is up and running, filled with content that adds value and *captures the email addresses* of those people who want more of your value-added content.

This is an old-school strategy that has worked for years and generated millions of dollars for countless marketers. Now it's your turn. Of course, you will be getting the "Brian G. Johnson" Trust Funnel variation of this strategy as we continue!

Once you've created an asset with your marketing blog, you'll want to continue to publish value-added content to your site as well as the big sites I keep mentioning. I'll share the very best way you can do this as we move forward.

By publishing content not only to your marketing blog but to YouTube, Facebook, Amazon, or Twitter, you'll end up driving traffic from these sites to your blog.

This will result in the following actions.

- Some will leave.
- Some will click on social "like" buttons or share your content.

- Some will link to your site as a valuable resource they want to share.
- Some will sign up for your mailing list.
- Some will buy products from you and your site via an affiliate link.

Understand that as we move forward, I will guide you on how to do these very things and/or point you in the right direction to ensure you're able to move forward. However, for right now, just understanding the basics of how your Trust Funnel will operate and what it should include will help you move forward in the right direction and in the right order.

All of these actions are incredibly beneficial for you and your Trust Funnel website, resulting in the *growth of an authority site* over time as the trend continues. After all, people will be linking, liking, and sharing your site content—all of which will drive additional traffic, boost trust and may ultimately boost rankings in Google. That certainly has been my experience.

Your mailing list will grow over time, providing you massive amounts of leverage. In a matter of minutes, I can drive thousands of people to any sales page, blog post, YouTube video or social status update I see fit. Even better, these are people that trust what I have to say and are interested in my opinions and recommendations. I'm able to do that because I've provided value for them. This allows me to promote my offers, affiliate offers, new content on my websites, and so much more.

Note: you're not going to focus on creating hundreds of little satellite sites, or use complex software to publish volumes of "average" content. Instead, you'll focus on real marketing strategies on "the big sites" with real users that are interested in what you have to offer.

CHOOSING YOUR TRUST FUNNEL NICHE

Because you're making a big commitment to the niche you choose, it's paramount that the niche you select is capable of generating enough income to satisfy your financial needs and wants. It's also important that you are passionate about the niche and able to create content that adds value. I personally believe passion is more important than knowledge; if you're truly passionate, you will learn, do, and teach. Understand that there is no "best niche" for everyone. The choice should be tailored to you individually.

Example: It's no secret that weight loss is a billion-dollar industry that makes plenty of people boatloads of money. Gardening and plant care is also a niche market with plenty of consumer demand; however, it's certainly not as lucrative as weight loss.

Your decision as to which niche market you choose should not be based on one single factor, such as consumer demand or the number of products that you can sell as an affiliate.

Sadly, for many people who are just getting started, this is the case. I see it time and time again. Choosing a niche is not about finding the perfect keyword phrase or simply choosing a niche based on the amount of money that is spent by consumers within the niche.

Rather, your decision to move forward and select a niche market should be based on the big picture, which includes a number of factors, such as:

- Your passion for a given subject
- Consumer demand
- Competition
- Personal knowledge
- Ability to demonstrate results (proof)

COMPETITION AND THE SIZE OF THE POND

These are the factors I recommend you look into and think over as you move forward with the decision-making process. I mention *big picture* because you want to think about *all of these elements together*. Now let's talk about the competition and the size of the marketplace.

While it's true that consumers spend less per year on gardening info products than they do on weight-loss info products, the competition in the gardening niche market will be substantially smaller than the competition in the weight-loss arena.

Thus, if you're passionate about gardening and have a lot of wisdom about the subject, it would be easy and enjoyable (imagine enjoying what you do for a living) for you to jump in, dominate the marketplace, and add value while also cashing in. However, if you were to follow the dollars and choose the weight-loss industry (a subject you really don't care about), you may struggle to come up with content that adds value for people, and without compelling content it's hard to achieve a high level of success.

For this very reason, when it comes to generating life-changing results, passion is something that you should think through before moving forward. Even better, find a niche that you're passionate about where people spend money, and you're golden!

COMPETITION AND COMMERCIAL INTENT

So often I see people worry about competition, wondering if they'll be able to compete, move forward, and ultimately get results in a competitive niche.

I can remember receiving an email from a potential customer that was filled with reason after reason as to why my program simply could not work, and this was why he was not joining me and hundreds of others who did (many of them made thousands of dollars just weeks after joining me that Halloween season).

One of the complaints he made was that, while there was lots of money to be made, students in my program would ultimately *compete with one another* in the same niche and earnings would take a dive as a result. This particular program was focused on driving Halloween costume sales via search engine optimization.

To the man's credit, that did actually happen. One of my star students actually targeted similar phrases as I did, and we started noticing each other's sites in the Google search results time and time again. I'll share our outcome in just a bit.

He also pointed out that all the sales (Halloween costumes) would dry up in the third week of October. This complaint proved to be unfounded. If this man had jumped in he would have learned that not only do people buy costumes all year long, but there are many surges throughout the year including November, when the discount shoppers buy (for the next Halloween season); New Year's Eve, when people buy costumes, hats, and accessories to celebrate; Easter (bunny costumes); and the Fourth of July (funky costume glasses and patriotic costumes).

Regarding the issue of taking sales away from one another, in my opinion this is simply seeing the glass as half-empty rather than half-full. What our opportunity seeker failed to understand was the sheer volume of sales that are generated every single Halloween season over the past five to ten years. Halloween is a $7-$8 *billion* dollar industry, with about 55 to 60 percent of that money being spent on costumes.

That particular program generated so much success for my students, and my star student at the time, Aidan Booth, and I often laugh at the fact that we showed up on the same Google results pages time and time again. Certainly we were competing with each other; however, we both made well over $20,000 in affiliate commissions within several weeks by simply seeing Halloween for the opportunity that it is. There is enough for everyone; it's an abundance mindset.

When it comes to competition, it's easy to find lots of reasons why something won't work. However, you'll never really know until you jump in and do it.

Personally, I always choose niche markets that are competitive. This is a sure sign that there is *money to be made*, and I always get a piece of that pie using my Trust Funnel tactics and strategies. You can do the same exact thing.

Fail-Safe Niche Market Criteria:
- Consumer demand
- Personal knowledge and experience
- Passion

Many people spend so much time on niche research, but research in fact means that you haven't even begun; rather, you've simply investigated the possibility. Let's explore how these three fail-safe criteria allow you to make an educated decision on which niche market you should enter.

FAIL-SAFE #1: CONSUMER DEMAND

Before a single word is written, before a domain is purchased, before you do any real work or pay anyone for anything, it's paramount that you know beyond a shadow of a doubt that there is **money to be made** in the niche market you're about to enter.

You'll do this by *identifying successful marketers* that are targeting *digital product* sales in the niche market you're looking to become a part of. This will allow you to move forward with confidence, knowing that you'll be establishing yourself in a market where there is plenty of money to be made.

Why should you pursue digital product sales, and what exactly are digital products?

Digital products are non-physical products that can be downloaded via the Internet. These include ebooks, reports, guides, software programs, apps for mobile devices, online membership sites, video training courses, and more. The cost of creating these products is incredibly low, and they can be sold at a very high profit margin.

Consumers are willing to purchase digital products for the information, knowledge, and wisdom they contain. Even more exciting is the fact that anyone with a PC can create a digital product relatively easily.

That last sentence is pretty darn important and where the excitement really begins.

Even more exciting is the fact that anyone with a PC can create a digital product relatively easily.

As an affiliate marketer you sell *someone else's* product and earn a percentage of the sale. However, by creating your own product, other affiliates can sell for you. And if you generate the sale for your product, you keep all the profits for yourself.

First you build your foundation as an affiliate marketer, focusing on establishing a presence with your marketing blog. You prioritize your efforts on traffic, building your email list, and selling other people's products as an affiliate. This will all be covered in the coming pages.

Later, if and when you're ready, you can take your marketing to the next level by creating your own product. Everything you've done to this point will help to ensure that your product launch is a success. You'll have a mailing list and free traffic, and you'll have built up presence and trust with many potential customers as well as product vendors.

Ultimately, you have assets that will work in your favor.

It's all about leverage and synergy, and again, if you don't want to launch your own product, you can still make substantial money by following the formula I've laid out here. I was a full-time affiliate marketer earning a great living and enjoying the freedom I desired for years prior to becoming a product vendor. How fast you move from affiliate to vendor is really up to you.

This is the power of focusing on digital product sales!

Identify Niche Markets Flush with Digital Product Sales

Just how do you identify *successful marketers* that are targeting digital product sales? The process is relatively easy and can be accomplished by doing some quick research of the platforms vendors often use to sell their digital products.

ClickBank is one of the largest digital product marketplaces and makes it easy for vendors to sell their products. The platform allows vendors to leverage a built-in affiliate tracking system, takes payment from customers, pays out affiliates who generate sales without any manual intervention, and more.

ClickBank also releases sales data of all vendors. This data makes it fairly easy to identify profitable niche markets.

Using the ClickBank Marketplace to Identify Profitable Markets

ClickBank offers a massive marketplace of the digital products sold on its platform. We can search this marketplace as we move forward to quickly spot niche markets flush with consumer demand. To get an idea, we'll use criteria that includes ClickBank gravity, vendor history, product price points, affiliate commissions, as well as the number of vendors who are servicing a particular niche.

ClickBank Gravity

This is a metric used to gauge the number of unique affiliates that have generated sales in the past twelve weeks. A higher gravity score indicates more affiliates have generated sales and that a product has a higher consumer demand.

Product Price Points

Understanding current price points in a given market can help to further understand profit potential; higher price points are usually an indication of consumer demand.

Affiliate Commission

Digital products often pay higher affiliate commissions (sometimes as high as 75 percent). Getting a general idea of typical affiliate commissions in any given niche market can help provide an idea of potential earnings.

Number of Vendors Servicing a Niche Market

The more vendors found operating within a given niche, the better; this is often a clear indication as to the consumer demand.

Simply analyzing these four criteria at CBEngine (www.cbengine.com) can give you a strong indication of consumer demand and profit potential. Let's take a look at how it's done.

Step One: Access the ClickBank Marketplace

Access clickbank.com and then click on the link for "marketplace" near the top of the page.

Step Two: Advanced Search
Once on the search page of the ClickBank Marketplace, you'll want to click on "advanced search." This will allow you to further define your search.

Step Three: General Search Term
Search the ClickBank Marketplace for a general search term. For example, if you're thinking about entering the weight-loss niche market, then searching for "weight loss" would be a great general search term that would return many different results on the topic of weight loss.

The goal is to identify the various products contained within a niche. Enter in your keyword phrase at the top of the search page, and search all categories.

Step Four: Refine by Searching for Items with Gravity Above
Right below the main search box you will see another search section titled "stats." Select "gravity" by clicking on the small box to the left of the page, and then select "higher than" and enter in "15." This will only return products (items) with a ClickBank gravity above 15.

The more vendors that show up on the search results page, the better. If you're *unable to find at least three or four* vendors that meet this criteria, I would recommend you select another niche market.

You may want to search a few keywords to identify various products that meet this criteria. If you're thinking about entering the weight-loss niche market, for example, you may want to search for:

- Diet
- Weight loss
- Muscle
- Aerobics
- Fit

Lastly, remember that the goal is to understand consumer demand in a given niche market and to further understand what digital products consumers are purchasing in the given space.

Assessing Demand by Spending Time on Popular Sites

Find the most popular forums and blogs within your niche market to get a clear idea of just how much demand your chosen market has. Ask yourself:

- How many people frequent the site?
- How vocal are the members?
- What sub forums are listed?
- Are any of the sub forums commercial in nature (for sale, service-based offerings, etc.)?

WarriorForum.com is a tremendous example. This particular forum is focused on Internet marketing, features a massive user base, and includes sections for the sale of products, services rendered, premium "paid" forums, and more.

Thus, one can make an educated assessment that the niche "Internet marketing" has tremendous consumer demand and also enjoys high commercial intent.

Check Out the Subculture

To reach potential site visitors as well as future subscribers, you're going to want to know what's happening in your potential niche market. Furthermore, niche markets all have their own unique subculture, language, and values.

Understanding and adopting the language they speak breaks down barriers and allows you to become one of them. After all, people like those they can easily relate to. Covering timely topics that affect a large percentage within your niche market addresses their needs and wants and breaks down barriers for you.

For example, online gamers have a language all their own, based on tech terms regarding the performance of hardware and software that power the games. Their language also is based on nearly a ghetto slang that is often spoken (or texted) while gaming. Login to any FPS (first-person-shooter game) and in no time you'll get a "WOOT! WOOT! I just owned you" and more.

Lastly, by spending time on the most popular sites, you may very well identify vendors who are earning and leveraging these sites to funnel traffic—and possibly sales to their own sites.

FAIL-SAFE #2: PERSONAL KNOWLEDGE AND EXPERIENCE

Internet marketing is a publishing business and thus your success or lack thereof is connected to the quality of *the content you publish and the value you add*. If you're drawn into a niche by the consumer demand but have little practical experience, you will most likely struggle with meaningful content creation.

Instead, why not identify subjects that have consumer demand as well as commercial intent (customers are not only interested in a given subject but are willing to spend). Do this by creating a list of subjects you have personal knowledge about. This may include any of the following:

- **What you do for a living**
- **A hobby**
  - Digital photography
  - Remote control cars and planes
  - Golf
  - Hunting or fishing
  - Gardening
- **A skill you learned years ago**
  - Calligraphy
  - Video creation
  - Cooking
- **Life experiences:**
  - Raising kids
  - Giving birth
  - Losing weight
  - Quitting a bad habit (smoking, drinking, etc.)

The items above are all great examples of subjects that would lend themselves to information product creation, and again, your list should be based on the subjects that you have personal knowledge about. It will be easier to publish content that addresses the needs and wants of your future visitors, subscribers, and buyers. Having personal knowledge of a subject is incredibly important. However, it's possible to enter a niche with little to no previous experience. I'll explain how in the next section, which focuses on passion.

FAIL-SAFE #3: PASSION

Ever since I was a young boy, I've been interested in computers, and being an entrepreneur. I often take on projects based on my personal passion and enjoyment of the subject matter as well as financial gain. Having lasting passion for a subject is vital for success. I have met very few people (if any) who have found a high level of success without truly loving what they do.

I also run incredibly hot or cold: I get inspired, interested, engaged, and can be very prolific with content creation—then later need an extended break. However, that passion for tech, the Net, and entrepreneurial success online has always been a big part of who I am. If the thought of writing articles, creating videos or audio podcasts is a hard pill to swallow, then I would urge you to reevaluate your plans for being an online entrepreneur.

The Journal Method and Marketing Blog

By now you understand that it's imperative to create compelling content that adds value for readers. As already mentioned, one of the easiest ways to do that is to choose a niche based on your own personal knowledge and experience. However, it is possible to enter into a brand-new niche, one that you know little about, and absolutely crush it over time. I call this the *journal method* and it works like gangbusters for one simple reason: The content produced is based on *personal knowledge* that is gained over time.

I first began teaching this method back in 2011 to a group of marketers. The idea was simple—select a niche based on the following:

- Digital product niche market
- Consumer demand
- Commercial intent
- The blog author's passion for a subject

As you can see, the criteria that must be met for the journal method is the same as outlined in this book. The goal is to enter into a niche that has consumer demand and commercial intent with consumers purchasing digital products, particularly information products (such as ebooks).

What's critically important is that the site author be truly passionate about the subject at hand. After all, these sites are intended to be long-term plays. For the journal method, understand that you need to research, learn, and internalize subjects to produce high-level content that adds value. These types of sites are great to launch when getting started with anything new in life that has consumer demand and commercial intent.

In fact, right now my wife and I are launching a blog on the process of building a house. As we go through the building process, we share our experience with others. In time the site will have lots of great content and will be an asset.

I like to think of journal type sites as little side businesses. Over time they will drive traffic, rank, and earn. However, the process can be a bit slower than entering into a niche you already have personal knowledge about.

Pen-and-Paper Research

Choosing a niche market to base your business on is really quite simple, and there is no need for fancy software that returns various statistics and metrics. Actually, this is exactly the thing you *don't* want to do.

Why? The answer is simple yet so often overlooked: As soon as you fire up one of the latest keyword software tools, the focus is on traffic and competition, and the amount of metrics and stats can be dizzying! While this type of data is important, it is NOT the most important element in finding success.

By far, the content you publish is the most important element, and this is why fancy tools are simply not needed (but can be helpful). Instead, grab a pen and pad of paper and write down those fail-safe points I mentioned above. Find that crossroads of where your personal knowledge meets with consumer demand and commercial intent—that is where you will find your niche market.

In the next chapter, we'll look at simple "pushbutton" methods and tactics you can use to quickly establish trust with Google. What I'll share is completely white hat and ethical, it will allow you to get off to a great start, and it won't take you any additional time or energy.

✔ RECAP:

Selecting a niche based on ***personal knowledge*** and your ability to create content that adds value, is absolutely key. Focusing on digital product-friendly niche markets provides additional leverage. You can easily get started as an affiliate and later become a vendor for added earnings.

🔖 HOMEWORK

Crossroads Research: Plan to spend a few hours over the course of several days to create a large list of your personal experiences and knowledge. Begin by examining the following areas of your life:

- Work, professional knowledge
- Life experiences
- Hobbies and interests
- How you spend your free time
- Things you're passionate about

Go through each one of these and create a list of all the subjects you have personal knowledge of and/or a great deal of passion about. Don't worry about consumer demand or commercial intent at this point. The goal is to create the largest list possible that will allow you to later sit down and assess each of the topics.

Later, when assessing the topics, remember to think about the big picture, taking into account the following:

- Consumer demand
- Commercial intent
- Ability to create content on a regular basis that adds value
- Your interest level and passion

All of the above items are critically important to your success. If you only follow the money trail (choosing a niche with massive consumer demand and intent), you may find that creating content that truly adds value does not inspire you, and thus you'll struggle to find success.

You can be a small fish in a big pond or a big fish in a small pond and earn life-changing income either way.

CHAPTER 6

PUSHBUTTON TRUST
AND TRAFFIC

I n this chapter we're going to *supercharge your marketing platform* for trust and success. As we move forward, you will be researching potential brand names, registering a domain, and securing social media brand URLs—laying the foundation of what will become your Trust Funnel.

The simple steps you take in this chapter will send a clear signal across the Web that screams authority and will greatly benefit your efforts. Some of these steps may seem like trivial decisions, but by addressing these issues now, your brand will benefit from consistent, congruent, authoritative, and professional wording and imagery with short, easy-to-remember addresses (URLs) that make it easy for visitors to find you on their favorite social platforms.

Example: MarketingEasyStreet.com

- MarketingEasyStreet.com
- facebook.com/MarketingEasyStreet
- YouTube.com/user/marketingeasyst

- twitter.com/MarketingEasySt
- plus.google.com/u/0/+BrianGJohnson-MarketingEasySt

Note: MarketingEasyStreet.com—Brand Name and Domain Length

I registered this domain back in 2011, and since that time I have gained a lot of wisdom about launching established brands and finding and registering those brand domains. I personally believe my domain is a bit long, and today I would have searched for something shorter.

However, my brand, MarketingEasyStreet, has also built up a lot of trust, links, social proof, and authority over the last few years. So I decided to stick with the brand for these reasons. If I had to do it over again, I would follow the exact blueprint contained within these pages.

BRAND RESEARCH AND CONSIDERATIONS

- Availability of a .com domain
- Availability of brand name across various social sites
- Easily identifiable for those interested or already in the given niche
- Offers a benefit to users
- Length of potential brand name (Twitter only allows fifteen characters)

Begin the process by focusing on the brand you will create; think short, memorable, easy to spell, and of course, available. If you're able to secure your own name as a .com address (no numbers or hyphens) I would suggest launching your platform in that manner. However, if like me you have a common first and last name, chances of finding a suitable .com will be challenging. Thus, you may want to move forward with a brand name instead, such as MarketingEasyStreet.com.

BRANDING FORMULA: THE ANCHOR METHOD

This is a simple formula that will guide you through the creation of a solid brand that is short, sweet, memorable, and easy to identify with—all of which are important to branding.

The anchor method allows you to create a brand name that is easy for the target audience to understand and "get" within a split second, and also it is benefit driven. That is, users experience a benefit only found with your brand.

Well, having a brand based on the anchor method makes it easier for you to describe what your brand is all about. And it's easier for the individual to understand.

If people don't get your brand, or if they don't understand it, **they will not move forward.** That's important because marketing is all about getting people to take action and move forward. Once you set up your Trust Funnel brand, you'll be asking people to move forward in all kinds of ways.

- Visit my blog.
- Check out this new product.
- Download this new report.
- Sign up to my mailing list.
- Share this post.
- Please leave a comment.
- Buy this product.
- Fill out this survey and provide feedback (actually two moves forward).

Thus, this method makes it easier to ensure more people "get it" and are in your Trust Funnel.

The anchor-method is based on incorporating two separate words or *anchors* into a brand name, and these two elements are based on the following:

1) A single word or two-word phrase that makes the brand easy to **identify and understand.**
2) **Benefits** the users gain with your brand.

Step One: The Identifiable Single Words List

Sit down away from the computer, get comfortable, and create a list of words that anyone interested or already in your niche market would instantly understand and relate to. Think of the high-level category type words. Since I'm in the Internet marketing niche, my list would look something like this:

- Marketing
- SEO
- Traffic
- Affiliate

- Blogging
- Blog
- Publish
- Publisher
- Social Media
- Facebook
- Google+
- Entrepreneur
- Tutorial
- Training
- WordPress
- Internet Marketing

For anyone interested or already in my niche market, the above list of words is easy to understand, identify with, and relate to. Furthermore, each of these words paints a clear picture of what a brand is all about.

BOOM! Winning!

You may want to include two-word phrases in your list as well. However, put your primary focus on single words as one of these words or phrases will become part of your brand name. The goal is *short, sweet,* and *memorable*; we'll need to modify the identifiable anchor word or phrase. This almost always results in the addition of *another word* or *additional characters.*

Step Two: Brand Benefit Anchor

Step two is all about the golden rule of Internet marketing: *Find out what people want, and give it to them.*

Take a moment and think about what's most important to your niche market.

- What are they looking for?
- What problems do they face?

Come up with a list of their wants and needs. Then create a list of benefits that address them.

Examples:

In my niche market, people turned to Internet marketing to make money, end of story. Today, folks who are successful got started not to blog or make videos or share on social media sites or self-publish books, but rather to cash in.

Thus, a major benefit that I like to focus on is the **money.** After all, my goal is to help people achieve their dreams and goals.

Another need and want for my niche market is *traffic*. Successful online businesses enjoy target traffic; it's the traffic that generates the money. Thus, another benefit I always focus on in my marketing is traffic.

Another want in my niche market is "easy," or a simple system that anyone can leverage to get results. Additional words that are related to systems include formula, blueprint, method, or ritual. All these words indicate a step-by-step process that generates a result. This is exactly how I came up with the name MarketingEasyStreet.com.

Next, create a new anchor list, this time based on the *benefits* that potential prospects will gain with your brand. Focus on single words or a phrase based on the benefits they are looking for. Let me also mention that you'll want to prioritize your list of benefits and focus on the most important ones.

Example:

I may talk about the power of Google Authorship, which can improve trust in a website, resulting in more traffic, which eventually will lead to money (the primary focal point of a potential prospect). However, I need to explain how the process works, and remember, if people don't understand, **they don't move forward and take action.**

Or I can offer a nine-step traffic formula based on proven and effective methods that drive more traffic, make more money, and just plain work.

Which one do you think people find more exciting?

Of course, a nine-step formula! One of the nine steps may be Google Authorship. However, by prioritizing the wants of my prospects, I can more easily get them to move forward with me.

My Benefit Anchor List:

- Formula
- Blueprint
- Ritual
- System
- Easy

- Simple
- Magic Bullet

Example Brands with Benefit Anchors:
- PushButtonSEO.com (pushbutton)
- SEOPressFormula.com (formula)
- MarketingEasyStreet.com (easy)
- CommissionRitual.com (ritual, formula, blueprint)

As you can see, many of my brands, including MarketingEasyStreet.com, are based on easy formulas that people can leverage to get results. That helps folks out, and it's the thing they are after as well.

People want a system or formula that simplifies the process and helps them to get what they want.

IMPORTANT!

It's easy to go overboard with claims and benefits. I see marketers do this all the time, and that's fine as long as you're able to *back up your claims*. Some things, however, you simply can't claim, such as guaranteed earnings, miracles, and so on.

If you make claims that are too good to be true, be prepared to deal with high refund rates and crazy people. After all, anyone with any common sense is going to pay little to no attention to an offer that clearly is too good to be true.

Proof is an important element when it comes to getting results, especially online. Be sure to show the results that you and previous customers have achieved using your brand and/or product.

However, it's vital to incorporate some disclaimers about earnings results (if you're in the "make money" niche market), and in the last few years the Federal Trade Commission has also been taking a hard look into testimonials. Testimonials must be written by real people and be based on actual results generated. I advise you to check with your attorney on the matter of disclosures, testimonials, and disclaimers.

THE POWER OF INCLUDING A FORMULA

A formula simplifies the process of achieving a desired result for a potential prospect. In a conversation with student-turned-master Aidan Booth, we spoke of the power of incorporating a formula anchor into a brand and/or product.

Aidan began telling me the story of when he was first introduced to me. It was on a webinar hosted by another very savvy marketer, Mark Ling, for my product, Commission Ritual. During the webinar, I revealed my simple nine-step SEO formula and went through each step in detail. Aidan later told me that his thinking at the time was: *All I have to do is learn this nine-step formula and I too can get similar results.*

A formula or system makes it easier for people to believe they too can get great results and that learning the system or formula will be fairly simple. Below I have included some of the brands I have launched. Notice they all contain both benefit and identifiable anchors.

Examples:

PushButton SEO: Anyone in the Internet marketing, WordPress, or SEO niches would certainly understand and identify with this name. "SEO" provides the identifiable anchor; "PushButton" is the benefit that users can expect with the brand.

Magic Bullet Books: In this case, the word "books" is the identifiable anchor and "magic bullet" is the benefit. That is, Magic Bullet Books will provide a simple formula or system that gets results easily.

Marketing Easy Street offers an easy-to-identify anchor and is also benefit driven, but, as mentioned, the name is a bit long.

So just what have I learned, and how will I create future brands that I launch?

Hard-and-Fast Rules:

- No domains over twenty characters (I suggest you shoot for under fifteen)
- .com extension
- Domain contains an identifiable anchor word
- No hyphens

Additional Considerations
- **How does the brand roll off the tongue?** PushButtonSEO, MarketingEasyStreet, and especially MagicBulletBooks roll off the tongue with ease.
- **How many characters are in the brand name?** Shorter is always better, never more than three words (and that's pushing it); two words are great.

- **Does the brand name have readability?** Type out the brand and domain names both with and without a .com, as well as with and without capitalization. How do they look? Are they easy to read? See the examples below.

PushButtonSEO.com
pushbuttonseo.com
Push Button SEO

MagicBulletBooks.com
magicbulletbooks.com
Magic Bullet Books
magic bullet books

WORD MASH—FINDING A SUITABLE AND AVAILABLE DOMAIN

The two-word lists (anchor words) you created above can be used to generate a variety of potential brand and domain names, and you can quickly and easily research all the potential combinations by accessing an online tool called bustaname.

Bustaname.com—Brand Name Generator

This free online tool combines lists of words, adds suffixes, searches for singular or plural variations, and mashes word lists together to create potential brand and domain names. It's perfect for creating domain names based on the anchor method.

SOCIAL ACCOUNT NAME AVAILABILITY

Once you have found a potential brand and domain name that is *suitable* and *available* to register, you'll want to ensure that the same name is available at the big social media sites including:

Must-Haves
- Facebook (page)
- Twitter
- YouTube
- Google+

You May Also Want to Register
- LinkedIn
- Pinterest
- Instagram
- Tumblr
- Flickr

CREATING A TAGLINE

Another choice is whether your brand and site will have a tagline. Many of my brands and sites have not had a tagline, and that is okay. However, you want to be thinking about this as you move forward.

The tagline should be very short, to the point, and further describe your brand and site.

Example:
PushButtonSEO.com
Tagline: Traffic Simplified

If you want to use a tagline, incorporate it across all your social sites as well as your website.

REGISTRATION: STEPS FOR SUCCESS

At this point, you have identified an anchor-based brand name that is both available as a domain and at the social sites.

It's time to register and make the name yours. Below I have included some best practices when it comes to registration of the domain as well as social media registration. Note that at this stage you'll only register a domain and social properties with your custom URL address. This way you will secure the address and it will belong to you.

1. Gmail Registration

First, before registering anything, register a Gmail address. You'll use this address moving forward to *register all other properties including your domain* and to manage your brand across the various social sites.

If your brand and domain name will be GooseRank.com, then register the Gmail address <u>GooseRank@gmail.com</u>. Furthermore, you will use "gooserank" when signing up and creating any custom URLs at the social sites such as Facebook, YouTube, and Google+.

This will make management easier moving forward (and let me tell you, things can get very complicated with multiple social accounts, different email addresses and whatnot).

Register your Gmail address here: Gmail.com

2. Domain Name Registration

I'm going to recommend that you:

a) Register the domain for a minimum of five years. This sends a message to Google that your brand and domain are a serious venture and may add to your site's trust level.

b) DO NOT register with domain privacy. Your site and brand have nothing to hide with Google, and again this may help to boost Google's trust ranking of your site.

TIP: SAVE WITH DOMAINCHEAPSTERS.COM
Save when you register your domain name with
DomainCheapsters.com.

3. Google+ and YouTube

Once you have registered your domain name, you'll want to register with two other Google properties, Google+ and YouTube.com.

Google+

Once you've signed in with your Gmail address, access the Google.com homepage. In the navigation located on the top right-hand corner, click the "apps" icon and then select Google+.

This will take you to the Google+ account that is associated with your brand. The first thing you'll want to do is fill out your Google+ profile. To do this access the navigation drop-down menu on the left of the screen and select "profile." Make sure you're viewing the page "as you." This will give you the opportunity to edit your profile. Do that by clicking on the "about" link.

Edit the content of this page by selecting the "edit" link that's found in the various sections of the page including:

- Story
- Word
- Education
- Places
- Basic Info
- Links
- Contact Info
- Contributor

Filling this out completely will help others interested in your niche market to find you and your website. Furthermore, Google+ is *crawled and indexed by the Google search engines*, and by using Google+ you can ultimately drive more traffic and make more money.

Your Google+ Profile and the Google Search Engine

While it should come as no surprise that Google+ usage can greatly impact search traffic from the Google search engine, adoption of Google+ by the masses has been slow. However, after spending considerable time researching current best practices for laying a solid SEO foundation, this is what I know:

Google+ features functionality that *no other social media platform* offers that can greatly impact your search traffic over time as well as your site's trust rank and authority—all great things that we'll talk about as we move forward.

1) Google+ Is Crawled and Indexed

When signed into a Google+ account, the Google search engine will often return Google+ results of those you are following. Thus, as more and more people follow you on Google+, your Google+ updates may be found by your followers when they use the Google search engine.

2) Google+ Authorship

Google+ Authorship allows webmasters to add a special code to their website that signifies to users and Google that the articles were indeed published by them (a trustworthy sign). The inclusion of this Google code impacts the Google search results by including a *picture of the author* next to the search listing. This factor alone is huge; the majority of Google search listings are text only. However, by simply adding a bit of code to your site (this will be covered in the upcoming chapter), your search listings will stand out and get more clicks, thanks to an image (as they say, a picture is worth a thousand words).

Furthermore, Google very well may favor sites that have incorporated Google Authorship in the future, even though currently Google says that authorship does not impact rankings.

This very book and Google Authorship are great representations of the new wave of SEO that is centered on establishing trust. *Trust rank* is a phrase that's been used for years by leading SEO authorities, and with Google Authorship we all have a chance to effectively plug into that trust.

Earlier I mentioned that Google+ was crawled and indexed by the Google search engine. With that in mind, you'll want to pay close attention to several of the fields you fill out on your Google+ profile.

Example of Google+ Authorship Google Listing

Story > Tagline:

The Google search engine uses what you enter here as a description (meta description) for your profile. Include a very short sentence or several phrases that describe what you're all about.

My tagline reads: *Serial Entrepreneur, Author, Speaker & Product Creator*

Google also uses the text entered into the "occupation" field to fill out your profile in the Google search engine. Thus, you'll want to add terms that are searched for often that describe further what you do.

My occupation reads: *Self-Publishing Expert, Blogger & Traffic Magnet—MarketingEasyStreet.com*

Links

Once your website is live and your social properties are up and running, we'll return to the profile page and specifically to the "contributor" section located under "links." This is where you'll set up Google Authorship; however, you won't want to do that until your site has a handful of value-added articles published to it.

3) YouTube Custom URL

Again, make sure you're signed into your Gmail account and access YouTube.com. You should see that you're signed into a YouTube account. When you first create a YouTube account you will have a default channel URL (web address) that looks similar to this:

http://www.youtube.com/channel/UCNimhyukHP5tdka3a9zi9Nw

However, you can easily create a custom URL based on your brand name that will look something like this:

http://www.youtube.com/user/YOURBRAND

To create your own branded, custom URL, access YouTube settings (located in the upper right-hand drop-down menu listed under your account name). Once on the YouTube settings page, click on "advanced" and then click "create custom URL."

Important: Take Your Time!

You can't make changes to your custom URL once it has been created; make sure to add your brand name and ensure that you don't make any spelling mistakes.

4) Facebook Page Registration

As we move forward I'll suggest that you use your personal Facebook profile as well as a Facebook "page." If you already have a personal Facebook account, simply sign in and access:

Click the little tool icon in the upper right navigation.

Select "create a page."

Select "brand or product."

Select "website" from the drop-down menu.

Enter your brand name where it says "brand or product name."

Once you get twenty-five fans of your new Facebook page, you'll be able to create a custom URL. I cover that as well as how to get those fans as we move forward.

5) Twitter Registration

Again, you'll want to sign up for a Twitter account with your Gmail address. Once you've signed up, you'll have a chance to create a custom Twitter URL for the account, just as you did with YouTube.

Other Accounts You May Want to Register

I've listed a few other accounts you may want to register with. This will reserve your brand URL at these sites. We'll talk about further customizing your various social accounts, publishing, and growing an audience as we move forward.

- Flickr
- Instagram
- Pinterest
- LinkedIn
- Tumblr

✔ RECAP:

- Brand names are powerful and can open the door and ultimately lead people straight into your Trust Funnel.

 HOMEWORK

- Register a domain name that's based on the anchor method.
- Register a Gmail account and use that email to sign up for the following social sites:
  - Facebook page
  - Google+ account
  - Twitter account
  - YouTube
- Register your brand domain Save at DomainCheapsters.com

CHAPTER 7

BONES OF THE
BRAND AND BLOG

n this chapter we'll continue to lay the foundation of your Trust Funnel, focusing on the visual aspects of your brand to ensure they are congruent with the messages you'll publish—that is, making sure your brand graphics, logos, and colors all capture the essence of what you're about.

You'll commission one or more logos that will unify the identity of your brand across the various social sites. You'll also get set up with a hosting account and have WordPress installed by your hosting company. Don't worry, I will provide you with step-by-step instructions on how you can optimize WordPress for Google searches.

SELF-HOSTED WORDPRESS WEBSITE

You have a number of options when it comes to the software you'll use to power your website. I highly recommend you go with a self-hosted installation of WordPress, and here's why: Not only is the software available for free, it is well supported and has become the leading platform in its space. Furthermore, WordPress is based on themes and plugins; themes control the look of the site and plugins extend functionality. Many excellent plugins and themes are available for free, and there are some paid options too.

As we move forward, I'll guide you as to what type of plugins you should use and *why* so you will understand *what we're trying to accomplish*. You'll have the option to test various plugins to achieve a desired goal. This will be much more powerful and give you options and flexibility as you build your Trust Funnel.

I will provide you with details on WordPress settings to maximize the SEO friendliness of your marketing blog as these settings rarely change. Plugins, however, come and go over time as new plugins are released, and some plugins are no longer as beneficial as they once were based on a number of factors (namely support of the plugin by developers).

If you're wondering if a self-hosted WordPress site is the right decision, know this: The vast majority of successful marketers use a self-hosted WordPress installation to power their sites. No other platform comes even close. Lastly, you'll be surprised to learn how easy it is to get started, and I'll hold your hand through each step of the process.

BUT WHAT ABOUT WORDPRESS.COM?

Before we move on, I want to mention WordPress.com.

WordPress.com is a hosted option that requires no hosting account, and while it's more turnkey and a bit easier to set up, it restricts the options you have available when it comes to themes, plugins, and configuration. These restrictions can and will jeopardize your ability to create a site that gets results, and this is why I strongly recommend you set up a self-hosted WordPress site.

Besides, you would be building the most important aspect of your Trust Funnel on someone else's site. That is a risk I would not advise.

WORDPRESS OPTIMIZED HOSTING

Not all hosting companies are created equal. I can't stress this enough. It's paramount that you select not only "the best" hosting for your website but a hosting solution that is tailored to the WordPress platform.

Another critical issue to address is support. Hosting accounts are generally "managed" or "unmanaged." You'll definitely want to get signed up with a managed account as they provide more support and can ensure your hosting account is kept up to date with the latest hosting technologies. Furthermore, when things go wrong with your hosting, you will have someone to call and speak to. This is critical.

I recommend you sign up with Liquid Web. They offer pushbutton installation of WordPress (if you would like to do it yourself) that will greatly simplify the task of getting your site up and running, 24-7 phone support, and leading server technologies that can improve site speed and ultimately Google rankings. I use Liquid Web myself.

Another excellent company is WP Engine. This hosting company is more expensive but is optimized exclusively for WordPress, and they have a stellar reputation.

I have created a detailed hosting review and social bonus offer at MarketingEasyStreet.com. You can access that information at: MarketingEasyStreet.com/hosting

CONNECTING YOUR DOMAIN TO YOUR HOSTING ACCOUNT (DNS)

Once you have a hosting account, you'll need to digitally connect your domain name to the hosting account. This will allow Internet browsers across the world to access your website. To do this you'll need to edit "nameservers" that are listed for your domain. Follow the steps below:

- Identify the namesevers associated with your hosting account. Most likely you will have received nameservers information via email when you signed up to your hosting account. If you are unsure, a phone call to your hosting company will provide you with the details you need.
- Login to your domain registrar (GoDaddy, DomainCheapsters, etc.) and access the domain name you want to install WordPress on. Next, update the nameservers to those that were provided to you by your hosting company. After you configure your nameservers it will take anywhere from six hours to several days (usually less than twenty-four hours) for the association between the domain and the hosting company to be live across the Web. Once the change has taken place, you'll be able to install WordPress onto your domain.

Okay, now let's walk through the steps to setting up your WordPress website.

1. WORDPRESS INSTALLATION AND OPTIMIZATION

Nearly all hosting companies will install WordPress on your behalf. Simply contact them via phone or their help desk and ask them to install WordPress for you. Or you may install WordPress yourself via your account's hosting control panel.

Both Liquid Web and WP Engine offer hosting control panels that give you the option of installing yourself. Furthermore, all hosting companies offer tutorial videos or how-to guides. You can also find tutorials on nearly every subject imaginable on YouTube.

Back up Email, WordPress Install Details to Yourself

Make sure to back up and save your WordPress install and login details. You might also want to look into using a browser add-on called "roboform." This hand browser plugin saves all user login info and is secure.

2. DELETION OF PREINSTALLED WORDPRESS CONTENT

Once WordPress is installed on your domain, you'll want to clean it up and begin optimizing the installation for Google searches. First you'll want to delete some preinstalled content that is simply a placeholder. This content is found on each new install of WordPress and includes:

* Hello world post
* Sample page
* Possible sample comment

Access this content and delete it. To do that, simply login to your new installation of WordPress and access "posts" and "pages." These are located on the left-hand navigation.

After clicking "posts," you'll be taken to a page that includes all the posts within the website (after installation you will see the default "Hello world post"). Simply hover over this post, and you will see several options including "trash." Click on "trash" and the sample post will be sent to the trash can.

Next you'll want to perform the same action for "pages." Again, click on "pages" and you'll be taken to an overview page that lists all pages located on your site. After installation you will see "sample page." Hover over "sample page" and again click "trash."

Auto-installed Plugin Deletion

Just as there is some pre-installed post and page content with each WordPress installation, there are also some plugins that offer no functionality. I recommend you delete them as well.

To do this, click on "plugins" on the left-hand navigation; doing so will take you to a page that features all the plugins available on your site. The plugin named "Hello Dolly" offers no real functionality and thus can be deactivated and then deleted.

3. CONFIGURING WORDPRESS SETTINGS

Now you'll want to ensure that your site's WordPress settings are optimized for Google search. Once reconfigured, some of these settings will make your site more search-engine friendly, namely permalinks.

Access the following settings by placing your cursor over "settings" in the left-hand navigation.

General Settings

Under general settings, make sure your "site name" is entered in the available field. What you enter here will be added to your site's header area if you do not use a graphic header. If you will be using a tagline for your brand and site, enter that in the "tagline" field.

WordPress Address and Site Address

In these two fields you should see the same exact address such as **http://yoursite.com**

Tip on Site Address Variations

Whatever is listed here is what you'll always want to use when referencing your site. Do not change the address to include the "www" as Google sees these as two different addresses. WordPress handles this just fine, and it's not a huge issue; however, consider this to be a best practices tip.

Email Address

Ensure that the Gmail address you created to manage your site is listed here.

The remaining site details can be configured as you like.

Writing

None of the writing settings are critical to the setup of your site.

Reading

On the reading settings you'll want to keep the default configuration for "blog pages" and "syndication feeds" to show at most ten. Under "for each article in a feed, show" select **summary** and not full text.

Discussion

You can keep the default installation settings under discussion settings.

Media

The media settings can be helpful if you want to tweak the thumbnail size of images or other image-related settings. I usually keep these set to default.

Permalinks

Permalinks determine the addresses for your site's posts. Furthermore, when optimized to "post name," your posts and pages will be far more optimized for the Google search engine as they will then contain words taken from the page or post name. Under permalinks settings, click on "post name" and save.

> **Example:**
> **WordPress Default Permalinks Post Address:** http://yourdomain.com/?p=128
> **WordPress "Post Name" Permalinks Post Address:** http://yourdomain.com/keyword-phrase-in-page-url

4. SETTING UP KEYWORD-DRIVEN CATEGORIES

Next you're going to want to set up a handful of categories that will allow you to organize the content you publish and further optimize your site for Google searches as well as the visitors to your site. First, we'll identify keyword-driven category names using Google's free Keyword Planner.

Step One: Get an AdWords Account

AdWords is Google's advertising network that allows individuals and companies to bid on ad placements for keyword terms as well as ad placements on websites in the Google AdSense network.

AdWords offers a variety of free tools, including Keyword Planner, which you'll use to identify various topics and the keywords Google searchers are using when searching for content based on these topics. You'll use these actual keyword phrases to create the categories for your site, resulting in a strong site hierarchy.

If you already have an AdWords account, login and access the Keyword Planner (located under "tools" in the primary navigation). If you don't have an account, you'll want to sign up for one now (free) at AdWords.com.

Once signed in, select:

- Search for new keyword and ad group ideas.
- Enter in a single word or two-word phrase that best describes your niche market.

Near the bottom of the page click "get ideas."

Example:

For my example site, BlogRankster.com, I entered in the single keyword "blog" and the Keyword Planner returned around thirty or so "ad group" ideas within seconds, including:

- How to Blog
- Make a Blog
- Blog Software
- Blog Design
- Blog Hosting
- Write a Blog
- Blog Promotion

To be clear, each of these "ad group" ideas contains various keyword phrases all themed together around a single topic, perfect for basing site categories on. You may want to go through this exercise several times to identify additional keyword themes and potential categories.

In my example site, BlogRankster.com, my niche market will be searching for "WordPress" as it is the leading blogging platform. Thus, by repeating the above steps, I uncovered the following ad groups and keyword themes based on WordPress:

- Learn WordPress
- How to WordPress
- WordPress Design
- Premium WordPress
- WordPress Plugins
- WordPress Themes

Lastly, create a list of five to ten categories based on the ad groups you discovered. Each category should be two or three words in length and no longer. Each time you publish to your WordPress blog, you have the option of creating either a post or a page. I recommend that you create posts rather than pages.

Posts are automatically added to your site's RSS feed (this is a good thing), and they are categorized using the category functionality. As we move forward with setting up your site, you'll create category navigation, making it easy for your future site visitors to find what they're looking for.

Step Two: Creating Your Site's Categories in WordPress
Login to your WordPress admin area, access the categories page (located under "posts"), and enter in your categories. Later we'll further optimize each category individually for the search engines after installing the SEO plugin by Yoast.

5. EXTENDING FUNCTIONALITY AND POWERING UP YOUR SITE WITH PLUGINS
Next you'll want to install plugins to add needed functionality that will create a better experience for your visitors and also help to boost your site's ranking in Google.

Depending on your theme, you may not need a plugin to achieve the desired outcome. Example, the list below mentions the need to create links in the footer of your website that direct visitors to legal pages such as Terms of Service, Use of Cookies, Use of Testimonials, and Contact Us.

Some WordPress themes will have this functionality built in, while others may not—hence the need to either find a plugin or hard code the theme yourself. Of course, plugins make it easy. Thus, first choose the theme you'll be using and then begin the process of adding plugins as needed.

SEO Plugin: All-in-One SEO or WordPress SEO by Yoast

Many SEO plugins on the market allow you to have more control over the title and description of the pages and posts you publish. This is the primary reason to add an SEO plugin such as Yoast WordPress SEO or All-in-One SEO.

I have used and recommend both; neither is any better than the other. Understand that Yoast is more feature rich and also much more complex; for this reason I recommend All-in-One SEO for those just getting started and Yoast for more advanced users.

Again, the functionality you want is the ability to add custom titles and descriptions to posts and pages you publish. Both of these plugins add an additional field on the WordPress editor screen as shown below. This is where you want to focus your energy.

Link Cloaking or Redirect Plugin—Pretty Links Lite

Anytime you promote an affiliate product, you'll want to track how many people click on an affiliate link from your site. You'll also want to create a redirect or cloaked affiliate link.

Over the years, Google has taken a hard stance on affiliate marketing, warning affiliates not to create "thin affiliate sites" which lack any real value for the end user. It's very easy for Google to identify a webpage that is promoting a product or service as an affiliate simply by analyzing the links on the page. Thus, it makes sense to create a special "redirect or cloaked" affiliate link that provides you more anonymity and does not give your "affiliate" hand away to Google.

How is Google able to identify these affiliate links?

Most affiliate links contain a common parameter that is found across an affiliate network. Let's take a look at ClickBank affiliate links, for example.

ClickBank Affiliate Linking Code
http://AFFILIATE.VENDOR.hop.clickbank.net

Any products or services available via ClickBank can be linked to using the above format, by including the affiliate and vendor username. Thus, right now online Google has identified millions and millions of webpages as "affiliate sales pages" simply by searching out the following link parameter:

hop.clickbank.net

In order *not* to get labeled an "affiliate page" you can easily create a redirect affiliate link that would not pass this affiliate link parameter. By using a link cloaking plugin, you can create affiliate links based on your own domain such as:

BlogRankster.com/go/pushbuttonseo

I like the free plugin Pretty Links Lite, although there are other links you may want to consider.

Social Plugins

Once your site is live, you'll want to add various social icons and buttons to your marketing blog that allow users to:

- Share your site as well as specific posts and pages on the social media sites.
- Access your social media properties such as your YouTube channel and/or Facebook page.

This is a great example of how the theme you select may already have social media elements well integrated. However, if you choose a theme that does not have social media elements well integrated, you may want to add a plugin or two to extend the functionality.

Some of the plugins I've used with success include:

- **Floating Social Bar**
  This is a plugin that loads quickly, does not slow your site down, and allows you to configure a social sharing bar that floats above the content as visitors access your posts and pages ... perfecto.
- **Social Pop**
  This is a little pop-up plugin that promotes your various social media properties as visitors land on your site. The end result is more and more people subscribing to your social media properties such as your Facebook page, Google+ account, and Twitter account.
- **Yet Another Social Plugin—Social Icons in Sidebar**
  You'll want to configure your sidebar with links pointing to your social media properties. This way people can easily find and subscribe to your various social accounts.
- **Facebook All Plugin—Facemash**
  Facebook allows developers (anyone who wants to mess with code) the ability to create what's called a "facepile" to add to their website. A facepile is a cool collage of "faces" of those who have liked your marketing website.

The end result is a graphic that lists the number of Facebook users who have "liked" your page and also incorporates their faces into the graphic. This is a powerful way to leverage social proof.

The plugin Facebook All makes adding this much easier.

Related Posts (WordPress-Related Posts—Zemanta)

People staying on your site longer and visiting more pages sends a strong message to Google that "people like this site." Furthermore, the more pages they visit the more likely they will "opt in" to your list, buy a product, and/or share or like a post or page.

Thus, you want to construct your site to encourage people to explore additional posts and pages on it. A related post or page plugin does just that and lists posts and pages that are similar to the one the visitor landed on.

A great plugin I've been using is called WordPress Related Posts by Zemanta. This plugin is pretty easy to install and also provides statistics based on how many people click to further explore your website.

Google Authorship Plugin

Google Authorship is one of the features that Google+ users get to take advantage of. Even better, a number of plugins make the process of setting up Google Authorship really quite easy.

I have been using a plugin called Starbox with much success. This plugin not only allows users to easily integrate Google Authorship, but creates a nice author box that can be included at the end of an article—powerful stuff that results in more traffic by incorporating your headshot into the Google search results as seen below.

Exit Pop Plugin

An exit pop plugin does what you would expect: It pops up when the visitor is about to leave and can generate a number of positive actions including:

- Building your mailing list
- Displaying your social media properties (and growing your subscriber base)
- Displaying a special offer for a product or service

These pop-ups work and they work well. Most exit pop plugins are paid. However, a few are free. Social Pop is one free plugin, and it allows you to link to your social media properties. Another plugin I've heard good things about is OptinMonster. You can learn more about various WordPress exit pop plugins here:

MarketingEasyStreet.com/access/exitpop

Footer Plugin/ Legal Page Footer Links/ Footer Putter

You'll want to create some legal pages on your site, including:

- Terms of Use
- Use of Cookies
- Use of Testimonials
- Contact Us

Search Google for "how to create a terms and conditions page" for further details. Once you have created these legal pages, you'll want to link to them from the footer of your site. This way they will always be accessible for anyone visiting your site.

Many themes make this process of adding links to a footer quite easy. If the theme you have selected does not, you may want to search for a plugin that makes adding these links to the footer of your site seamless. One such plugin I have used is called Footer Putter; it's a free plugin and works well.

Optional—ManageWP

Expect bumps in the road with your website; sooner or later it's bound to happen. ManageWP is a service and plugin that allows you to:

- Schedule backups of your website automatically
- Update plugins and themes for multiple sites from one central location
- Track your site and protect it from hackers and viruses
- Track your site's Google rankings
- Clean up your site's database to improve performance
- And lots more

ManageWP is available as a free service (at the time of this writing) and can also be upgraded to a paid account to extend functionality. I use this service myself. When something terrible happens, I know I have website backups at the ready.

Highly recommended; you can learn more about ManageWP here:

MarketingEasyStreet.com/access/managewp

Optional—PushButton SEO

In the coming pages you'll access my Trust Funnel Ranking Formula that will guide you through the process of publishing content optimized for Google searches.

I created PushButton SEO, a plugin for WordPress, to allow people to easily publish content via WordPress that is optimized for the search engines. This plugin has incorporated the exact steps found in the upcoming Trust Funnel Ranking Formula and thus will ensure your content is optimized.

You can learn more at:

PushButtonSEO.com

Working with Widgets and Optimizing the WordPress Sidebar

Widgets are another component of WordPress that allow further configuration and customization of a website. There are thousands of widgets available, and each adds different functionality to a site, such as listing recent comments, listing categories, adding in a calendar, pulling in quotes, having the ability to add in text, and lots more. Depending on the theme you use, you can add various widgets to different sections of your site.

Common Widget Areas:

- Sidebar
- Header
- Footer

Some premium themes offer additional widget locations including the site's homepage and/or site feature area. After you play around with widgets and understand the basics, you can further tweak your site as you see fit.

How to Configure Widgets and Your Site's Sidebar

To get started, login to your WordPress dashboard, hover over "appearance" and select "widgets." This will take you to the widget page. On the left side you'll see available widgets that you can literally drag and drop into the various sections of your theme (located on the right of the widget page). All themes offer the ability to drag and drop widgets into the sidebar. This is what we'll focus on.

Clean Up: Widget Removal

First, clear out any widgets already installed in the sidebar. To do this, simply drag the widgets from the left and drop them into the right section of the page. Once you're done, you'll have a nice clean slate to start from (no active widgets in the sidebar).

> In this next step I'll guide you through the process of optimizing your sidebar to instill trust, begin to grow a social following, call attention to recommended products, and develop and display social proof over time as your audience grows. All of this can greatly impact the success you're after, and it all begins with *which widgets* you display and *where you display* them.

In the image below, you can see how I have configured my sidebar based on the steps I'll share with you. The order is very important, and each widget and where it appears is calculated.

The Listing Order of ...

Optimizing
Your Website
Sidebar

1) Author Headshot Widget and Bio Welcome

Author Headshot Widget

At the very top of your sidebar, you'll want to include a headshot of yourself as well as a very short bio or tagline. The picture should be the same photo you're using for your Google+ profile picture.

Doing this instills trust and confidence, and here's why: A large percentage of your visitors will find your site via a Google property such as Google Search, Google+, or YouTube. Many of these visitors will have noticed your profile picture. Remember that your Google+ profile picture is featured on all of the Google properties.

Thus, when they land on your site and see a welcome bio and the *same picture* they just saw at YouTube, Google+, or Google Search, that builds trust and confidence.

Your picture will also allow people to get a sense of who you are and what you do. Once again, this very act of sharing a bit about yourself via a picture builds trust.

There are many plugins and widgets you can use to create an author bio. Remember to use the same picture that you use for your Google+ profile, as this builds familiarity.

A very simple solution I have used with success is to create a "Google+ Badge" which uses your Google+ picture and also links to your Google+ account. You can do this yourself by searching Google for "google plus badge" and selecting colors, sizes, and copying the code.

Next, pull the "text" widget from the left of the widget page over into the top position of your site's sidebar. Open up the widget and paste in the Google+ Badge code, and you're set.

Social Icons — Yet Another Social Media Icon Plugin (YASIP)

In the second position of your sidebar, you'll want to feature icons that link to your social properties such as your Facebook page, YouTube channel, or Twitter account. Many plugins allow you to do just that. At the time of this writing, I'm using Yet Another Social Media Icon Plugin (YASIP).

Installation is fairly simple. Begin by downloading and installing the free plugin. Once the plugin is active, you'll see a new widget appear that you're able to pull into your sidebar. It's also possible to configure the plugin with the social sites of your choosing.

Advert #1

Use the third sidebar widget to link to a product to generate a sale, include an opt-in form to build your list, or highlight a blog post that you want to drive additional traffic to. You can use an affiliate banner or creative by simply copying code into a text widget once again. The goal is to push more traffic to wherever you want and whatever will benefit you the most.

For example, at the time of this writing I have just launched an ebook to the Amazon Kindle store. Thus, I created a widget that included a cover image of my ebook and a link to a blog post about the ebook, effectively this has driven more traffic and thus sales of my ebook.

Facepile or Similar

In the fourth widget position, I suggest you incorporate a social media element that leverages social proof. A great example of this is available from Facebook and, as was previously mentioned, is called a "facepile." Again, a facepile graphic displays the total number of people who have liked your marketing blog and also displays many of their faces as well.

This sends a clear message to new visitors: "This is a popular and well-liked site." This is to your advantage. Of course, when you first launch your site and Trust Funnel, you won't have many likes. However, over time that will change as more and more people find your site. You can manually create the code needed to add your own "facepile," or you can leverage the YASIP plugin that makes the process a bit easier.

Popular Posts / Recent Posts / Comments

Next, incorporate a popular posts plugin.

- It highlights your best content.

Oftentimes, these plugins also show the number of comments made by others on the posts themselves. This is another form of social proof that is very powerful.

Some premium themes have a popular post widget already integrated; OptimizePress 2 is a great example. However, a number of other plugins also allow you to add this functionality to any theme.

Advert #2—Optional

This is a second advertisement widget area where you can push traffic to where you want it to go, allowing you to build a list, sell a product, or display advertising. This widget area is optional, and if you're not sure what to include, just skip it.

Categories

Categories

Categories
Affiliate Marketing
Branding
Case Studies
Coaching
Colorado
Confrences
Domain Names

This widget area lists all the categories of your website, allowing site visitors to easily find what they're looking for.

The "Do Not Use" Widget List You want to avoid duplicate content across your own website (this recommendation comes from Google by the way). Many of the available widgets add navigation that will ultimately increase your site's duplicate content. These include:

- archives
- tags

Since you've already added the category widget to your theme, there is no need for either of these widgets; **do not use them.**

6. BRAND LOGO, HEADER, AND SOCIAL MEDIA GRAPHICS

All right! You're nearly done setting up the bones of your blog. You've added plugins that will add functionality, improved the SEO factors of your site, configured your sidebar to instill trust, increased social proof (which will build over time as more people find your site), and ultimately put together a well-oiled machine.

However, *machines do not drive traffic and sales.* Great content and the human personalities behind it are what drive traffic: trust and sales. This is why the next step is critical. We're going to ensure that your site stands out from the crowd, looks professional, and has a human element.

The very best plugins, widgets, and WordPress themes cannot accomplish this, and it's often overlooked. In fact, it took me years to truly see the power of branding, which begins with the creation of a great logo and graphics pack that will power the *look and feel* of your website and social media profiles.

A Picture Is Worth a Thousand Words

The header image you slap onto your site and social profiles will separate you from the tens of thousands of competing sites across the Internet in either a good way or a bad way. Within a split second of landing on your site, people will begin to make judgments, and by having a professional looking header, you can make a great first impression, which of course can lead to further trust.

Your header and logo should convey what your brand is all about. If you're in the Internet marketing or SEO space and your brand creates plugins and themes for WordPress, you may want to go with a clean, sharp tech look. PushButtonSEO.com is a great example.

However, if your niche is dog training, you may want to go with something a bit more playful, perhaps based on a cartoon logo. I would very much encourage you to add images of yourself to the header or cover graphics you create.

After all, much if not all of the content you publish will come from, well …YOU. Thus, it makes a ton of sense to have some professional pictures taken. In early 2014, I hired a professional photographer in my city to take some shots of me.

Graphics + Your Picture = Win

I'll use these images in my header logo across my social sites as well as in blog posts, Kindle ebooks, social media updates, and more. While it does cost a bit more to get professional shots taken, the quality really stands out and will separate you from the majority. If you're willing to spend fifty bucks for a theme or a plugin, think about spending up to a few hundred dollars for some professional images.

Note: I want to point out that with Trust Funnel and the creation of your marketing site, the goal is to gain authority and expert status, drive traffic, build a list, and promote various products. However, what you're building IS NOT a product site or sales page. Branding, logos, and graphic headers for sales pages are very different in that they usually don't include picture elements and are much cleaner in appearance—putting the focus on where it should be, the marketing message (sales video, sales letter, etc.).

Basic Graphics Needed to Get Started
Your marketing site:

- Logo and/or header
- Footer (optional)

Facebook:

- Profile image
- Cover image

Google+:

- Profile image
- Cover image

Twitter:

- Profile image
- Cover image

Next Step: Commission Graphics That Incorporate Your Logo

After you've gotten back your professional photographs (if you'll be using photos in your headers and social graphics), the next step is to hire someone to create the headers and social graphics you'll need.

Use the above list to create a detailed document that highlights all the graphics you'll require. I suggest you hire a designer that specializes in social media graphic design. They will already know and understand dimensions for all the social sites.

Have the same person create all the needed graphics, with congruency throughout. That is, all the graphics should look the same, use the same color palettes, and include the same logo.

Hiring a Graphic Designer, and Other Available Options

You have lots of different options (and of course price points) when it comes to graphics work and social media branding. Below I've highlighted some of the services I've used with great results. I've also included tips to ensure that you get great results as well.

TweetPages.com

Matt Clark is the designer behind TweetPages as well as ImageDesigns.com and can provide you with a simple, professional, and creative solution that's designed specifically for your brand. Matt has designed for dozens and dozens of A-list marketers. Highly recommended. You can learn about TweetPages here:

MarketingEasyStreet.com/access/tweetpages

99designs.com

Another option is to create a design contest at 99designs. The process is straightforward and will result in a variety of different designs based on your needs. I've used 99designs for Kindle ebook covers as well as for logos.

Fiverr.com

Fiverr is an amazing marketplace that I've personally used to outsource graphic design work at very reasonable prices. However, since the price points are so low, it's critical to know exactly what you want and be specific with those you hire.

The more details you're able to provide the designer, the happier you'll be with the end results (this is especially true when using a low-cost solution such as Fiverr). Before you contact anyone to do design work, you should have a basic idea of what you want.

- Color palates
- Logo
- Will your graphics include a tagline?
- Fonts
- Will your photo be included within the graphics?

Fiverr Tip: Hire three separate designers for your project and have them design one element, such as your site header. Once you get the designs back, ask your favorite designer if they would be interested in creating similar designs for YouTube, Facebook, Twitter, and Google+. This will still keep the price you pay incredibly low but will also allow you to see and judge custom design work from several designers.

HOMEWORK

- Get a hosting account
- Change your domains DNS to point to your hosting account
- Have WordPress installed on your domain (or do it yourself)
- Set up keyword-driven categories
- Install needed plugins
- Configure and optimize the sidebar of your site
- Acquire needed headers and/or logos for your brand

CHAPTER 8

EXPERIENCE-BASED SOLUTIONS— THE BLOG LAUNCH

This is where *we* pivot. This is where winners attack and leave their mark while others flounder and wonder why they struggle to get results. I can't stress it enough: The results you achieve (or not) are based on *what you publish* and the *technologies you leverage to publish.*

However, understand that *what you publish* is ultimately what leads to the results you're after. The technologies merely allow you to get those messages, videos, blog posts, and social updates in front of more people, and it all starts with your marketing blog and what you publish there.

Your marketing blog is the start and center of your publishing platform, and in this chapter I'll show you how to optimize that content for the visitors to your site and for Google as well. Thus, the end result will be a growing stream of traffic from all the big sites that matter. With that traffic, you'll be able to build a list, promote products, and ultimately get results.

BLOG POST END GOAL

Each and every time you publish to your blog, your goal should be based on the following:

- To add value, inform, and educate people based on the topic at hand
- To optimize your post content for Google as well as social media sites, resulting in a stream of FREE traffic that will grow as you build your brand and continue to publish

By addressing BOTH of these items you'll be creating synergy and people will find your value-added content and subscribe, share, like, comment, and basically *engage* (all of which helps to establish you and your blog as an expert in your field, leading to additional FREE traffic and ultimately success).

Of course, some blog posts will do better than others; however, by consistently adding content and leveraging the other big sites to market your blog content (this will be covered as we continue) you will get results and traction.

I know, for I have followed these exact strategies many times over with great success.

ANCHOR CONTENT AND EXPERIENCE-BASED SOLUTIONS

There are various strategies you can implement to create high-quality content that gets results, and one of those methods is what I like to call the Anchor Method.

This is a critical component that will allow your content to rise above the competition and stand out in a very noisy Internet and ultimately hook readers— ka-BOOM!

The Anchor Content Method demonstrates that you have what they want: high-level thinking and strategies as well as *personal experience* with the very issues they are facing. Your strategies and experience can ultimately help them solve the problems they face day to day. Furthermore, the Anchor Method demonstrates *with actions* that you truly want to help your subscribers and future buyers get results.

What actually is anchor content?

Anchor content is *any* content published to the Web that goes far above and beyond the typical. It could be a blog post, a YouTube video, a paid membership site, or a free report that results in praise and accolades from the target audience.

In the case of your marketing blog, anchor content will be in-depth posts created with one singular goal of delivering tremendous value to visitors. This is also known in the marketing space as "pushing the free line." The idea is simple:

You give away quality content that your competition would charge for. That's the hook.

When creating and adding an anchor post, the goal is simple …

> 👍 Use anchor content to add *tremendous amounts of value* for people. Notice I did not say "add value" but rather *tremendous* amounts of value!

Anchor posts are typically much longer than a normal post and often contain one or more types of media which may include:

- Videos
- Audio files
- Interviews
- Infographics

Above all, anchor content demonstrates your *personal experience* and provides solutions to common problems that others face. Understand that even if you're just getting started in a given niche, you can still share your personal experience. As long as you're sharing *personal-based solutions as well as what you've learned*, you will be creating compelling content that brings people back.

That being said, strive to be the best you can be and to provide people with solutions to their problems. Always be learning and striving to become the best you possible.

I can tell you for certain that I have become a much better marketer based on the products I have created and sold over the years. I work at it a bit harder, understanding that I have more on the line (people who will access my materials and depend on my methods).

Important:

Don't be under the impression that you have to be perfect with your teaching; make it your aim to help others succeed, and let them know you've experienced some of what they're going through. No matter the niche or subject, find the pain point and provide an experience-based solution.

- How to get rid of mealybugs (orchid care)
- How to optimize a blog post (SEO)
- How to approach a woman or man (dating)
- How to trade on the foreign currency exchange (FOREX)
- How to lose weight and eat chocolate (weight loss)

Begin the post by explaining what's in it for the reader as well as how you can help and why the reader should listen to you. That last part is important, especially when you're just getting started, as nobody knows or trusts you (yet) online.

You need to tell them why they should listen to you and trust you.

And this is where the philosophy of playing your hand should be implemented. Don't think for a minute that you don't have something to offer. Instead, play the hand you've been dealt the best you can. If you've got years and years of experience with the subject, you're the vet. If you're brand new but incredibly passionate about the subject, and you've already experienced success, play the "newbie" card. Since I've been full time for many years, I play my hand as the expert, full-time marketer, coach, and mentor.

I do this with videos, blog posts, sales letters, etc.

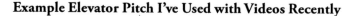

> **Example Elevator Pitch I've Used with Videos Recently**
>
> *Hey, Brian G. Johnson here, #1 bestselling Kindle author, engaging speaker, product creator, SEO expert, poodle wrangler, and all-around good guy …*
>
> *I've used the Kindle platform to build a list, gain exposure for my brand, sell books, and ultimately create a residual-based revenue stream that hits my bank account month in, month out—all thanks to Amazon and Kindle.*
>
> *In this video I want to share how I've leveraged x-y-z to drive more sales, get more reviews, and ultimately make money using the Amazon Kindle platform.*

USE OF IMAGES TO LEVERAGE YOUR PERSONALITY

You'll want to use some engaging images that grab people's attention. Images can and should be based on the topic at hand, and if your anchor post is based on a solution such as "7 ways to stop mealybugs from destroying your orchids," then any type of graph, chart, or data-based image can go a long way. In this case I would think about finding these types of images to use:

- Close-up gross picture of a mealybug
- Picture of a happy, healthy orchid plant
- Graphic type image with a bit of text: "7 solutions to stop mealybugs"

Another great option is to feature you in the image or picture and simply incorporate some text that gives insight into the topic of the article. This way you're building your own brand and people will come to know, like, and trust you.

I used the image above to promote a speaking engagement where I gave a talk on Kindle self-publishing. However, the image featured me and the simple text message "the worldwide premier" of Brian G. Johnson's Wealth War Cry. I've successfully used similar images to promote my blog posts or anchor content.

Also note that people will find your content as they search for solutions. You can educate them and they will return; however, if you can entertain *and* educate, more people will return, share, subscribe, and generally want to be a part of what you're all about. People are bored and have little to no attention span, so anything you can do to spice up a video, blog post, or product launch should be used.

Furthermore, it makes the process of creating this type of content so much more fun! In the past I've used pictures of Al Pacino, Captain Kirk, and other witty imagery to express my goofy personality, and the feedback has always been great. Just remember why people are reading or watching your content. Focus on the golden rule (what they want) and entertain at the same time and you will be setting yourself up for success.

Speaking of the golden rule, think about all the issues that are important to your potential customer and site visitors, and address them often. The key is to prioritize their wants and needs. Start the process off by creating a list. Once the list is complete, then prioritize their needs and wants.

In my case, what's important to my market is the following:

- Money
- Traffic
- Simple and easy methods

These are pretty much the top three wants and needs; thus, I tailor all my messages (blog posts, videos, and products) to address this list *in this order*, and you should do the same.

If you're just getting started or are not happy with current results, you'll want to leverage the power of the Anchor Method. Here's why: You need to convince people that they should follow you and read your emails, blog posts, and social media updates. ***This is where your Trust Funnel begins***, by pushing the free line and demonstrating you have what it takes and that your content, methods, and strategies work.

In the fall of 2013, I attended a workshop held by Rick Butts that inspired some of the hooks for this very book. During the workshop I learned about three items that must be addressed when speaking:

- Clarity
- Control
- Courage

Your message must have *clarity*, you must be in *control* while delivering that message, and you need to have the *courage* to move forward and do it! Be sure to address these "3 C's" any time you publish content to the Web, with the end goal of having someone do something:

- Opt-in to a list
- Buy a product
- Leave a comment
- Etc.

I'll be the first to tell you that I struggle with these, especially clarity. I'm terribly longwinded and sometimes struggle with delivering a focused message. However, this is something I'm working on all the time now. It's vital that you be crystal clear with your messages and your "call to action" (all content should include a call to action in some way, shape, or form), which we'll cover as we move forward.

While at this same event (by the way, go to events!) Rick often mentioned "stealing the ball" from your competition, and that's exactly what anchor content does. It highlights your content above others, and when you're pushing the free line it ensures that the barrier to entry is reduced to nothing (lots of people will learn what you're all about).

Lastly, don't worry about giving away too much for free. Think long term and know that lots of people will want your paid content as well; and when you over-deliver with your paid products you will create a customer base that buys from you over and over.

Results of Anchor Content I've Published

1. Happy New Year's—WordPress SEO Tutorial Video Series

During the first or second week of January 2014, I posted a series of comprehensive tutorial videos on WordPress SEO for 2014 and covered installation from start to finish with around a dozen or so videos. This was my project for about a week, and I treated this blog post as a paid product.

The results were tremendous, and I was able to help and support many people with the content. I delivered value and gave it away for free and got attention (hard to come by online). The post also enjoyed a ton of comments, social shares, and likes across all the big sites (free traffic I would not have had).

2. How Not to Suck at Internet Marketing

This was a "heart-to-heart" type post, written from me to my readers. It was funny, creative, and based on actual encounters with a potential buyer who wanted to have "guaranteed results" before moving forward and buying my product.

It was an important message, and I took my time to craft it the best I could. The results were again tremendous.

Here is how the post got started:

For the last ten months I have been focused on "Going Big," and if you want Internet marketing success, if you want to be able to generate revenue online, then this blog post is vital information that you must understand.

The Internet Marketing Smoke Job

If you screw this up, you will fail, mark my words. If you try to cheat the system, again, you will fail. If you think your black hat, super spinner, auto-posting, "build ten thousand links in a snap" approach is the solution, allowing you to lie on the coach, eat potato chips, and watch reruns of *Hogan's Heroes* as your $37 wonder software builds your empire, then put the hookah pipe down and wake up: You too are going to fail miserably.

3. Commission Ritual—Paid Product

Here is an example of where truly over-delivering and adding value with a paid product can bring attention to what you do.

In 2009 I launched Commission Ritual, a product that resulted in more than a quarter million dollars in profit for me and took my business to the next level. I spent my time creating the product. It had many modules covering various aspects of traffic generation, WordPress, SEO, and affiliate marketing and was centered on *experience-based solutions* that only I could provide (my methods, my training).

I wanted people to truly get value for their money, and I achieved that goal. The images below are not testimonials but actual customers' responses from the largest Internet marketing forum online.

While these examples demonstrate that I put much time and thought into the content I posted, realize that most people do not and that the bar is set fairly low. You don't need to film fifteen videos or spend months on a project to have an impact and get noticed.

You simply need to add value by sharing your experience-based solutions.

MEDIA ELEMENTS TO INCLUDE AND TYPES OF ANCHOR POSTS

The Power of Video

Many strategies and tactics can be used to create value-added content. Below I've included some of these strategies that I've used with much success. First off is video. Once you begin to create and leverage video, doors will open up due to the power of transcription as well as how video makes it easy for people to connect on a deeper level. This leads to trust and a side benefit of people spending more time on your site—a great thing in terms of SEO.

If you're thinking *nope, I don't want to do video*, please stay open to the opportunity and possibilities that video can offer and instead clarify that statement.

- I don't want to put myself in front of the camera.
- The technical details scare me.

There are numerous video creation methods you can leverage, and chances are strong that if you open yourself up to *saying YES to video* you will find one or more video creation methods to use, apart from getting in front of a camera. However, I will mention that doing just that can have a powerful impact on future results.

Some of the video creation methods I use are: interview-based video, tutorial (screen capture) video, welcome video, product review video, sales video (not used for blog content per se) as well as story-based "lessons learned" video, news and update style video, and more. In the upcoming chapter on video marketing I'll cover these video creation methods in more detail.

Two Birds with One Video (and Other Media)

Before I move on to the next content creation strategy, I want to mention one powerful aspect of video as well as other multimedia including audio, slide presentations, and more. Multimedia, and specifically video, can stand on its own when hosted on sites like YouTube, and it can ultimately drive traffic as well as build and draw attention to your brand.

Furthermore, multimedia can easily be incorporated into your blog post content, thus you can strike two birds with one stone. This gives you a chance to target twice as many keyword phrases—once on your blog and once again when you upload a video to YouTube.

Audio—Podcasts, Audio Interviews

People love to watch *and listen*. While video is great at instructing folks who are actively engaged in front of a screen, audio allows them to take it with them. Millions of people (including myself) listen to downloaded audio while driving, working out, traveling, and more. And when they listen, the amount of distraction is reduced big time; you have their complete focus and thus a chance to really connect.

Anchor post audio content could include an audio program featuring yourself, someone you interview, or a recording from an event you attend. Audio formats can include simply uploading a single audio file (usually an MP3 or AAC file) that you include in your post or a more structured podcast format distributed via iTunes. Note that many WordPress plugins make the process of including audio fairly easy.

Surveys, Metrics, and Statistics

People love numbers, lists, and statistical information, and you can use information that's already available online to create a powerful stats-based anchor post.

Flowchart Anchor Post

Flowcharts have been used for ages and can easily be incorporated into an anchor post that helps users to understand a process and/or concept in a visual manner.

Flowcharts can be made online or by using software such as MS Word, Excel, or Pages.

Slide Presentation

A slide presentation is a powerful way to captivate an end user, and they can be used in multiple formats to drive traffic, build a list, and increase sales.

Most of the time, when I launch a product, I create a webinar presentation based on a PowerPoint or Keynote file that I use. You can use the same strategy to create and record via video slide presentation that you later upload to YouTube and include on your website. For an added boost, also upload the actual slide file (PowerPoint or Keynote) to SlideShare and link to the blog post. This is a great example of cross-promotional strategies that we will get into as we move forward.

Infographics and Illustrations

Humans are incredibly visual creatures, and in a noisy Internet world you need to do everything in your power to capture someone's attention. Images will help you do that.

With each and every anchor post I launch, I include a handful of high-quality images. I pay a monthly fee for a subscription to Big Stock Photo that allows me to download ten images a day. This is great as I can use these images in Kindle books, headers, images for blog posts, infograpics, and lots more.

Several other online sites make the process of creating quality infographics possible. Learn more about various free online graphics sites here:

MarketingEasyStreet.com/access/easy-graphics

Live Events with Google Hangouts

This is yet another example of video, this time with the ability to go live if you like and invite others to attend, interact, ask questions, and more. Google Hangouts is part of the Google+ family and integrates deeply with YouTube. I am moving forward with this medium to increase exposure and interact with others in a fun way that goes beyond the typical blog post.

How can you use Google Hangouts for an anchor post? There are a number of ways. You could set up a live video conference with industry peers to discuss the niche market you operate in. You could interview established leaders and experts within your niche market. This is actually easier than you may think if you approach people at the right time. As they say "timing is everything," and if you approach a marketer who is launching their own product, they will be much more interested in spending time with you on video.

This can result in traffic, leads, and affiliate sales. Video marketer and all around great guy Zane Miller has done this on several occasions with very good results, and in the process he has become known as the Video and Google Hangouts guy. Michael R. Thomas uses a similar strategy and, little surprise, has also made a name for himself by springboarding off of "successful Internet marketers." Michael did this simply by setting up Skype video interviews that he recorded and then posted to his site, Mike from Maine.

Since Google Hangouts is deeply integrated with YouTube, after the live event is over you can easily embed the video replay into a blog post with a transcription of the video itself. This gives readers two options: They can watch or read. It also provides Google with lots of text content to crawl and index.

> *I want to go off the cuff right now and point something out. This is a great example of people moving forward with proven and effective methods that work. In this case, two great marketers increased their exposure simply by leveraging video and interviewing the right people at the right time.*
>
> *Success is not hard to find; you just have to **make a plan of action** that is **best suited for you,** and you need to show up, take action, and keep pushing the ball forward. Success is easy once you understand that it's not found in a bottle, a pair of jeans, a WordPress plugin, or software suite.*

Q and A Blog Post

The question-and-answer method once again returns us to the golden rule: *Find out what people want, and give it to them.*

Steve Scott is a popular blogger and avid Kindle publisher (wicked smart of him as Kindle is a tremendous source of buyer traffic) who has leveraged the Q&A format wonderfully. This method requires you to get feedback from readers, visitors, etc.

It may not be the right method to leverage if you're just getting started (feedback will be hard to come by). However, once you get some traction with readers, this is a wonderful strategy to put into play.

First, post to your blog asking readers for feedback and what they would like to learn from you. You might post something like this:

What would you like to learn about and have me cover on the topic of _____ (insert your niche topic here). I'm planning on creating one heck of an in-depth post, and I would love to help you with any issue you may have.

Next, email your list and include a subject such as:

I'm answering your questions ...

Link them to your blog post, then address and answer each question the best you can. I plan to leverage this method myself in the very near future and intend to use video. What's great about this method is that:

1) You're asking what your readers and subscribers need help with.
2) You're truly adding value at a high level, and that will be demonstrated by your actions when you follow up with an epic anchor post designed to help others—with no "buy" button in sight.
3) You may learn about topics that you would not otherwise have thought of.

Like any anchor post, you must go the extra mile. When you think you're about done, answer two more questions, and if at all possible also include media (video, audio, infographics).

Trending Topic-Based Theory or White Paper Anchor Post

This method allows you to leverage a trending topic, which can result in added traffic, exposure, a bigger list, and more. As I write this very book, a flurry of activity has busted out on Facebook. My peers are crazily discussing whether

Klout matters (Klout is a social media site that scores marketers based on their activity on various social sites such as FB, Twitter, Google+, and a few others).

Friend E. Brian Rose, one of the founders of JVZoo.com, posted a status update that posed the questions "Does it matter?" and "What do you think about Klout?" He also tagged about twenty highly visible marketers, and what ensued was forty-eight hours of nonstop chatter and buzz on the subject.

This would have been a tremendous opportunity to post an in-depth theory-based blog post covering the subject of Klout, how to leverage the metric, and more. With so many people busily focused on the subject, this type of blog post would get lots of added exposure via Facebook or wherever the news is trending.

Once again, I cannot stress enough the importance of going deep and digging into the subject matter:

- What is it?
- Does it matter?
- Why does it matter?
- How can you improve your score?
- What should you not do?
- What are the positive aspects?
- What are the negative aspects?
- Can you provide a guide of sorts ("how to do _____")?

And I would turn to video as it's the one media that touches on the most senses; that is, people can:

- Hear it
- See it
- Watch it
- Feel it

STEP-BY-STEP STARTUP GUIDE

One of the best groups to target is newbies or those just getting started with any given subject. After all, much of what you can share and cover in a "startup guide" will be new information and extremely helpful to those just starting out.

This type of guide can be created by any marketer, whether you're brand new (newbie card) or a seasoned vet with years of experience. Simply play your hand and move forward.

To create a startup guide, formula, or blueprint post, begin by listing all the factors that matter in a given subject and then prioritize them based on importance. Lastly, create a numbered "step-by-step formula or blueprint" such as:

- Brian G. Johnson's Six-Step Kindle Formula
- The Nine-Step Ritual Ranking Formula

Doing this helps me to get better results by automatically prioritizing my actions, and it allows those just getting started to focus on what matters. Include one or more of the following: flowchart, infographic, tutorial video or audio. Lastly, name the post based on a numbered system as listed above. For example:

"Discover the Six-Step Kindle Formula and Crush It on Amazon!"

"Easily Rank in Google with the Nine-Step Ranking Ritual!"

Topical Comic Post

Jared Croslow has leveraged the power of comics and cartoons to poke fun at the Internet marketing industry, and the result has been tons of links back to his site, and fame. Jared's cartoons were fun, and most people in the Internet marketing space related to the topics he covered. That made his site stand out. You may not be a budding artist; however, with sites like Fiverr, it's possible to outsource a creative idea that can help to draw attention.

HOW OFTEN?

Ah, the age-old question: How often do I need to blog?

Here's the short answer: *as often as you can, but no more than you want or need.*

Understand that when it comes to Internet marketing, you will always have a million various tasks to spend your time on. Prioritizing your efforts is key, and you will want to keep a running tab of "what I must get done today, this week, etc."

That being said, when you launch your marketing blog, you will *need* to make it a priority! Once your blog goes live, it will have zero content and will provide zero value to anyone who should find it—until you add a handful of anchor posts.

The good news is that you can and should plan it out and have content already written before you launch your marketing blog. This is especially true if you're just getting started with WordPress as it will make the process of creating a true asset easier.

LAUNCH YOUR MARKETING BLOG AND ANCHOR CONTENT

Step One: Creating the Text Content

Always begin with the priority, which in this case is the content. Focus your energy and attention on simply creating the text content that your first anchor post will feature. Plan it out; think through what types of anchor posts you want to launch with and what topics you may want to cover. Launching with three or four anchor posts is fine, and once the site is live you can add other content as you see fit.

I advise you to keep things **really simple** early on. Doing so will help to ensure that you're always moving forward in creating an asset. This is especially important if you're brand new to online marketing as you will be learning lots of new things all at once.

The first goal is to *launch and optimize your WordPress marketing blog* and to upload five or six posts with great content not found anywhere else. And there is no reason why you can't focus on audio or video elements later, after your site is online.

If things seem overwhelming to you, then focus on simplicity. Choose the topic you're most excited about and make that your priority until the text content is complete. Then move forward with a second topic, using the same strategy of selecting what you're most excited about at the time. Once you have written out your three or four anchor posts, you can move on to finding the images you will use with each post (each post should have a minimum of one image and no more than five). Make sure you can use the image before you post it online; you can do this by checking the image license prior to posting.

Step Two: Optimizing Your Posts and Adding a Call to Action

When posting to your blog, you'll want to address a couple of items.

- Identify a long-tail keyword phrase that you'll optimize your content for.
- Add a call to action to the post itself.

First you'll want to identify what's called a *long-tail keyword phrase* that people are actively using while searching Google—one that is relevant to the actual content.

What the heck is a long-tail keyword phrase, and why are we targeting it?

A long-tail keyword phrase is four to seven words in length and more descriptive of what the searcher is actually trying to find; it's usually a bit easier to rank for as well (a very good thing indeed).

Examples of Keyword Phrases and Long-Tail Keyword Phrases

Keyword Phrase: *Hosting Coupon*

Long-Tail Keyword Phrase: *Hostmonster Hosting Coupon Code*

Let's take a look at each of these keyword phrases in regards to SEO competition in Google (how competitive it is to rank for a certain keyword phrase) and the ability to convert the visitor into taking the desired action (buying, subscribing, commenting, sharing, etc.).

At the time of this writing, the keyword phrase "hosting coupon" returns fifty million Google results. Fifty million! That's a lot of pages showing up for this phrase, and the number of companies and marketers that are targeting "hosting coupon" I can assure you is massive. The keyword is very popular and certainly drives a lot of traffic, but it's important to put yourself in the shoes of the searcher and dig down to what they really want. What we know about this Web searcher is that they want a hosting coupon.

However, there still remains many unknowns that the searcher may or may not know themselves. For example, are they in need of a Windows or Linux server? Are they a power user or just getting started? Since we do not know these answers we can't tailor the content and message on our marketing blog to this criteria, and thus conversions will be much lower.

Remember the Golden Rule: *Find out what people want, and give it to them.*

When it comes to the second searcher, we know that not only are they searching for a hosting coupon, but they are after a specific coupon for Hostmonster, and they want the "code" as well.

Thus, we could easily tailor an anchor post to feature a detailed sales message focused around these very precise items that the search is after, which in turn will generate a higher conversion rate and ultimately earning more money.

Also note that the long-tail keyword phrase "hostmonster coupon code" has 157,000 results, a mere fraction of our other example. Lastly, this exact phrase has earned me tens of thousands of dollars in affiliate commissions over the years. Bottom line: It makes a ton of sense to focus on these types of keyword phrases. Identifying a long-tail keyword phrase is quite easy, and I cover that in the coming pages.

Now, let's discuss how to actually publish the content using WordPress.

POSTING YOUR ANCHOR CONTENT WITH WORDPRESS

To post your content, simply login to your WordPress dashboard, select "posts," then "add new" and you will be taken to the WordPress editor. The editor offers lots of flexibility and functionality that will allow you to easily format text and incorporate images as well as other media such as video (and more). How you edit the content and where you add your target long-tail phrase has a huge impact on Google search results.

WordPress Publishing 101

When on the editor page, you will see the following:

WordPress Title Field

This field produces the WordPress post or page title, which shows up on the actual page as an H1 or H2 heading. Page headings carry a fair amount of weight with Google in terms of SEO; thus you'll want to incorporate your long-tail phrase as mentioned below in the Trust Funnel Ranking Formula.

The WordPress Formatting Toolbar

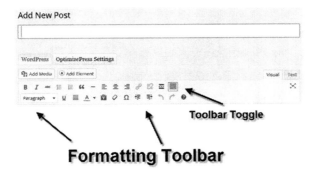

Right below the title field you will see the formatting toolbar with the simple buttons that allow you to select bold, italics, strikethrough, create bullet list or numbered list, add a block quote, align the text, insert or remove a link, use the more tag, enter into the free write mode, and lastly, the toolbar toggle button, which reveals even more options.

Text and Visual Editor

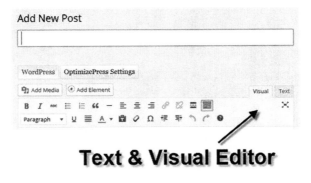

When formatting a post or page, you can do so in either the visual editor or the text editor. When using the visual editor, changes you make will appear as you work. However, in the text editor you will see the code that generates the changes. Thus, it's much easier to format a post or page in the visual editor.

WordPress "Add Media" Button

Located right above the formatting toolbar, you'll find the "add media" button. This is where you'll upload images for inclusion in your post content.

WordPress SEO by Yoast or All-in-One SEO

After installing either the All-in-One SEO or Yoast WordPress SEO plugin, you will find a new field that allows you to enter an HTML title and description for the post or page you will be publishing, both of which are located in the actual code of the page.

Note: The HTML title and description are different from the WordPress title and carry much more weight in terms of Google ranking power.

You'll find this field below the main edit content area. As mentioned, the HTML title and description are found in the *code of any post* or page you will publish, and both carry a tremendous amount of weight in the Google algorithm and thus can go a long way in helping you to rank well in Google as well as the Bing search engine.

WordPress SEO by Yoast

General | Page Analysis | Advanced | Social

Snippet Preview (?)
marketingeasystreat.com/?p=4238

Focus Keyword: (?)

SEO Title: (?)

Meta Description: (?)

The meta description will be limited to 156 chars. 156 chars left.

All in One SEO Pack   (?) Help

Upgrade to All in One SEO Pack Pro Version

(?) Preview Snippet

http://veganblogger.com/?p=1053

(?) Title

0 characters. Most search engines use a maximum of 60 chars for the title.

(?) Description

0 characters. Most search engines use a maximum of 160 chars for the description.

Both plugins will guide you through the process of creating optimized titles and descriptions and will provide an example of what the post or page will look like when listed in the Google search engine.

OPTIMIZING YOUR POST FOR THE SEARCH ENGINES

This is where most people stop. That is, they don't think about how to optimize the content they publish to appeal to both human visitors and the search engines. However, the moment you begin to think of publishing for both groups, you will have a massive advantage over those that do not.

Warning: Analysis Paralysis, Info Overload, and Time Wasted

It's so easy to get caught up in trying to craft the perfect post for the search engines. I've seen this happen time and time again. People lose sight of what's most important, and that is:

To add value for real people who are interested in the topic you are publishing about.

When writing this very book I struggled with which SEO plugin to recommend. Yoast is powerful and offers much more customization, and thus it's far easier to get overwhelmed, confused, and to spend far too much time "optimizing."

Do not do it.

There is far more value in focusing your efforts on *another piece of content you will publish* that will add more value for people. Instead, understand that you simply want to be mindful of what's most important to Google and what makes the Google algorithm tick.

Remember, we're prioritizing our actions.

This is *exactly* why I created the 12-Step Trust Funnel Ranking Formula (along with my own SEO plugin). Follow the twelve steps and you will publish content that's Google friendly and addresses the needs and wants of real people.

All-in-One SEO itself has more than enough options to keep you busy if you're just getting started. Make use of my twelve-step formula and the All-in-One SEO plugin.

The Yoast SEO plugin will guide you through the process of crafting a well-optimized post and also help you to identify the *target long-tail search phrase* mentioned above.

If you will be using the All-in-One SEO plugin, you can easily identify a long-tail search term by simply typing in one or two words that best describe the article you will publish. As you type in these words, Google will provide "search suggestions" based on what others have searched for.

To dig deeper, search Google once again for a primary keyword phrase such as:

how to tie a tie

Then scroll through and add a letter from the alphabet such as:

how to tie a tie a

how to tie a tie b

how to tie a tie c

You can do this in a minute or so, and in the process uncover hundreds if not thousands of potential long-tail keyword phrases. Always choose the phrase that most *accurately describes what you will be publishing.*

Lastly, you may want to consider a keyword software tool that provides additional metrics such as SEO competition and more. Learn more here:

MarketingEasyStreet.com/long-tail-software

Let's dive into the twelve steps of my Trust Funnel Ranking Formula. That's the subject of the next chapter.

CHAPTER 9

12-STEP TRUST FUNNEL
RANKING FORMULA

A s you publish content to your site, simply follow these guidelines and you will address what's most important with Google.

1. 100% UNIQUE CONTENT THAT'S
NEVER BEEN PUBLISHED PRIOR

What you publish to your site must be 100 percent unique content that's never been published and is not accessible anywhere else online. Also, the content must not be available to anyone else. This is an important one; the chances of you ranking well for content that has already been published (or will be published by others in the future) is greatly diminished. Lastly, once you publish this content you won't want to publish it anywhere else online. This way, the only way Google can share this content is on your website. It will be the one place across the entire Internet that it can be found. Simple and powerful.

2. 1,000 WORDS, MINIMUM

Note that you do not need to post a thousand words or more each and every time you post to your blog. However, statistically speaking, Google tends to rank longer articles much better. Thus, when you *really want to rank* for a given keyword phrase, post longer articles—one thousand words, minimum, with as many as twenty-five thousand.

3. IDENTIFY THE "TARGET" LONG-TAIL PHRASE VIA YOAST OR GOOGLE

After you've added all your text, image, and media content, you'll want to identify your long-tail keyword phrase, which can be done right from the WordPress edit dashboard. To get started simply access the general tab area of the WordPress SEO by Yoast (below the post content area) and enter in a keyword phrase that best describes the article you're about to publish in the "focus keyword."

Once you've added a keyword phrase, you'll see additional keyword phrases based on the term you've entered. Select the term that best describes the content, and remember that longer keyword phrases are usually easier to rank. The keyword phrase you select will be your "target long-tail phrase" and will be used often in optimizing your post or page content.

4. INCORPORATE THE TARGET LONG-TAIL PHRASE INTO THE WORDPRESS POST OR PAGE TITLE

Create a post or page title that incorporates your long-tail phrase.

5. CREATE A PERMALINK BASED ON
THE EXACT TARGET LONG-TAIL PHRASE

**Create a Permalink
Based on the Long-Tail Phrase**

Also known as the URL, the permalink is the actual Web address of the post or page you will be publishing, and it's very important when it comes to SEO. The permalink should be the exact long-tail phrase as pictured above.

6. BEGIN SEO TITLE WITH LONG-TAIL PHRASE

Begin your SEO title with your long-tail phrase and you're set. Note that you have seventy characters to work with and you can include additional keyword phrases that relate to your post or page as well.

7. BEGIN THE DESCRIPTION WITH THE TARGET LONG-TAIL PHRASE

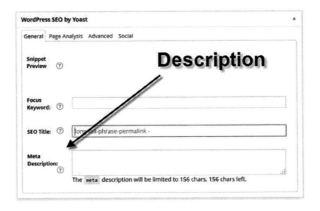

As mentioned above, the description field is very important as Google will usually pull the data found in the description field and use it when listing your post or page on the Google search engine. Thus, you want to make sure to begin the description with your long-tail phrase and at the same time write a description that someone wants to click on from Google to visit your page.

8. INCORPORATE THE TARGET LONG-TAIL PHRASE IN THE FIRST FIFTY WORDS

You'll want to work your long-tail phrase into the first fifty words of the post or page.

9. INCLUDE THE TARGET LONG-TAIL PHRASE IN AN H2 OR H3 TAG

Also known as headings, you'll want to include one or two H2 or H3 tags that contain all or some of the words found in your long-tail phrase. Add in H2 or H3 headings via the WordPress editor, first select the "toolbar toggle" and then on the bottom left of the toolbar you'll see an option for including "Heading" to your post.

10. INCLUDE THE TARGET LONG-TAIL PHRASE IN "ALT IMAGE TAG"

Add your target long-tail phrase to the "alt tag." This HTML tag provides a description about an image in text format. This way if people have images disabled in their browsers, they'll get an idea as to what the image is about based on the alt tag.

11. LINK FROM OTHER PAGES ON YOUR SITE USING SOME OF THE WORDS IN YOUR TARGET LONG-TAIL PHRASE

How you link to various pages and posts across your website can greatly improve ranking while also providing navigation that helps visitors to find the type of content they want.

Thus, creating links from other pages and posts across your website to the current page will help to drive results in the future. The related post and page plugin that you installed earlier will help to do this automatically, but you should still make it a habit to interlink posts and pages across your site.

12. INCORPORATE AN OPTIMIZED CALL TO ACTION IN ANCHOR POST CONTENT

A call to action is simply the act of telling readers what they should do next. This can include any of the following:

- Buy
- Subscribe
- Like or share
- Comment

Any time you post content to the Web (not just on your blog), think through what action you want viewers to take. This could include leaving a comment, signing up to your mailing list, buying a product, or sharing your content.

This single step can improve your marketing many times over. If you don't tell someone what they should do, usually they will do nothing.

Oftentimes marketers incorporate banners and sales graphics to their sidebars and stop there. Or they might add a subscription widget or sales banner advertising with a WordPress plugin. In my testing, these types of ad displays get a very poor conversion rate, almost always less than 1 percent. I still add them to my sidebar, as it does help overall, but by also including an "optimized call to action" you can greatly increase your results. Site visitors are far more likely to read and process an optimized call to action due to their placement.

Even if you're not promoting a product or service, still incorporate a call to action that may include:

- Add a comment
- Share this post
- Hit the like button
- Sign up to learn more

These various calls to action will result in the growth of your mailing list, visitor engagement, social proof, and more.

OPTIMIZED CALLS TO ACTION

Since people will be focusing their attention on the content area of your marketing blog, this is exactly where you want to add your call to action.

Furthermore, the call to action should be a natural extension of the post content itself, and when you do ask the viewer to buy, subscribe, share, or comment, the conversion rate will greatly improve.

When creating content to sell a product or service, you can put a number of additional tactics into play to improve the conversion rate yet again. I'll cover these in detail in the upcoming chapter on affiliate marketing.

You'll want to add the call to action in every form of content—that is, if you're creating a video, make sure to tell people in the actual video what they should do. When you post text content to your blog, again, tell them what to do (in text form).

Be sure the call to action is very visible on your marketing blog. Use a larger font, increase the point size, or use a graphic to make the call to action stand out.

VARY THE CALLS TO ACTION

The content you publish to your marketing blog should have various goals, including:

- Entice the visitor to opt-in to your list.
- Entice the visitor to buy a product or service.
- Entice the visitor to share, comment, or engage with you.

If you're not trying to sell anything, but rather simply over-delivering and adding value for your visitor, your goal should be to get the visitor to demonstrate that the content you provided was helpful in some way. Don't be shy. Ask them to share your content and/or leave a comment. This will result in additional traffic, social proof, and/or further reciprocation at a later date and time.

Thus, different posts and pages on your site will benefit you in different ways.

- Some will build your list.
- Some will drive traffic via social sharing.
- Some will increase your social proof element.

By varying your calls to action you will not always be asking people to buy, buy, buy (this can annoy and aggravate some site visitors).

Examples of Various Calls to Action
In the coming pages, I'll provide a real life example of a call to action on my marketing blog that has generated thousands and thousands of leads for my business.

Optional Step 13: Create and Include Video and Other Multimedia

Once you're comfortable creating an optimized text and image blog post or page, you'll want to add another tool to your marketing toolkit. I recommend you first focus on video as it's more powerful and will allow you to leverage YouTube (the second largest search engine on the Web) to drive traffic and build up another subscriber base that you can interact with.

Adding a video to your blog posts and pages also results in people spending more time on your site and gives them a chance to get to know you more easily; after all, video can be seen, heard, and felt.

Keep Readers Engaged: Marketing Phrases
Another great way to catch and keep people's attention is to incorporate colorful marketing phrases into your blog posts and pages. These words and phrases can be incorporated into titles, headlines, and text content.

The following list was created for my own internal use in the Internet marketing niche; however, it can be applied to other niche markets as well.

- Automated System
- Growth and Moneymaking System
- Set It and Forget It
- Unleashed on the Marketing World
- For the First Time
- This Page Could Change Your Life Forever
- Rake in $_____ in his first month
- Newbie Cracks the Code
- Uses the Ugliest Website
- Can Make You
- Mind-boggling
- Attention Online Income Seekers
- Most Effective
- Step-by-Step Moneymaking
- Start Using 15 Minutes from Now
- Guaranteed to Work
- Put in an Hour or So Per Day
- Fastest, Easiest and Most Profitable
- ClickBank Outsider Returns Sheepishly
- Revealed
- Extract Huge Sums of Cash
- Simple but Powerful Method
- Extract More Money from Any Website
- Instant and Unlimited Access
- Right Now
- Legitimate
- Decent Profit Margins
- Pre-Screened
- Real System to Pull $500—$1,500 Per Day
- Working from the Comfort of Your Home
- Moneymaking Info
- Exposed!
- "Breakthrough" and "Groundbreaking"

continued on next page…

...continued from previous page

- Revolutionary Internet Marketing Technology
- Finally Get a #1 Google Ranking in as Little as Seven Days
- Drive Unique Visitors to Your Website
- Discover the System That Created an EXTRA $___ in Less Than 14 Days
- On Autopilot
- Double, Triple, and Quadruple Commission
- A Big Honkin' List
- Monster Paydays
- Financial Travesty
- Works Wonders
- How to Make Money
- The Gurus Never Teach
- Real Money Exchanges Hands
- Churning Out Behemoth Fortunes
- Beat the Gurus at Their Own Game
- Time to Turn on the Power
- Push Button
- Quietly and Consistently Making Six-Figure Income
- A Way to Make Money That Has Never Yet Failed
- Amazing True Story
- Revolutionary Profit-Predicting Software
- Instantly Uncovered
- Sure-Money Affiliate Program and Keywords
- Plug in and Profit Today
- If You're Not Using XXX, You're Leaving Money on the Table Every Day
- Anyone Can Use This to Start Profiting Today
- The Only Way to Fail Is by Not Taking Action

continued on next page...

...continued from previous page

- You Can Be Financially Free Within 6-12 Months Delivers Month After Month Income
- Completely On Autopilot!
- STOP Chasing After the Gold
- Become a POWER Shovel Seller
- Big Boys Make the Big Money
- Maximizing Your Conversions
- Just Got a Whole Lot Easier
- Discover the Amazingly Simple Secrets
- Exactly How I Made $____ in 37 Days
- How You Can Too
- The BIG System to Making REAL MONEY
- Finally Succeed on the Internet
- Turnkey Money Machine That Prints Non-Stop Profits
- Automatically, the Lazy Way!
- Rake in Up to $__ per Day
- Set Aside Just One-Three Hours Every Week
- Let Me Show You How to Get Cash in the Bank
- Hands-Down
- No-Debate
- Easiest Way to Make Money Online
- Proven Effective Way to Promote Your Affiliate Link
- Stop Being Held Hostage
- Send You Checks Every Month
- Taught Thousands What to Sell Online
- How to Create a SERIOUS Income
- Unleash a Torrent of Dependable Profits
- Richest Trading Markets the Financial World Has Ever Created
- Do It Securely ... with Minimum Risk
- Get Expert Help Every Step of the Way

continued on next page...

...*continued from previous page*

- It's Not Too Late
- Remember When You Thought You Could Achieve ANYTHING in Life?
- What 99% of the Population Doesn't Know Is Quietly Changing Those Who Do
- Something Fantastic Happens Every Day at the Same Time
- It Will Make You Rich
- Learn the One Hidden Secret
- Make an Incredible Profit
- This Secret Will Completely Change Your Life
- All You Need Is the Idea and Exact Trading Algorithm
- Virtually No Competition
- Traffic Espresso "Double Shot"
- Blasts Your Organic Search Results
- Hundreds of Backlinks
- Closely Guarded Goldmine for Many Super Affiliates
- Heavy-Hitters
- Consistently Nailing Incredible Rankings Over and Over Again
- Power to Legally Exploit
- Rapidly Rank for Virtually Any Keyword
- The Actual Loophole to Systematically Get #1 Rankings
- Finally Exposed!
- Easily Earn More Than You're Making in Your Full-Time Job Right Now!
- Step-By-Step, No-Fluff Blueprint
- Drop All the Time-Sucking Manual Labor
- Get Your Hands on a Long-Lasting Passive Income

continued on next page...

...continued from previous page

- Stream Auto-Created Profitable Niches
- Secrets to Working From Home
- Making Money on the Internet!
- Kiss Day Job GOODBYE
- Make More Than $__ per WEEK Working from Home
- Magically Money Starts Pouring into Your Pocket!
- Stop trying to give me a fishing pole, just give me the fish—seriously!
- Breathtaking Internet Success
- It's Something That Truly Works
- Your Day Job Is Tougher Than Ripping Thousands of Bucks from ClickBank Every Week
- What Happened Next Almost Floored Me
- "Knock Me off the Chair and Leave Me Gasping for Breath" Floored Me
- Brutally Effective Underground Moneymaking System
- Slumdog to Millionaire
- Dominate the Playing Field
- True Paint-by-Numbers System
- Massive Profit Windfall
- Powerful Money-Sucking Profit Streams
- Leverage Free-to-Use Web Properties
- Make More While Working Less
- Affiliate Strategy Manipulates Google
- When Revealing How Much Money It Makes, You Probably Won't Believe Us!
- Fastest Way to Generate Extreme Profits
- Frankly It DESTROYS Any Other Type of Marketing
- You'll Be Truly Blown Away

continued on next page...

...continued from previous page

- Suddenly Realize Just How Much Money You Can Make All Done in Minutes on Autopilot
- Want to Discover How We Made $__ in 30 Days?
- Copy Every Last Online Moneymaking Secret We Have
- Unlimited Supply of High PR Backlinks
- Laser-Targeted Traffic
- Tap into an Unlimited Supply of Targeted Traffic
- Secret Blueprint to Online Wealth
- Give You This Same Secret for Next to Nothing
- Give Yourself an Unfair Advantage over the Competition
- The Million-Dollar Blueprint Results Are Shocking!
- Legally Steal My Most Secret Blueprint
- Ever-Growing
- Finally Hand You a Proven System to Making Money
- You MUST Follow a PROVEN Plan
- "A" to "Z" in Building Your Businesses from the Ground Floor Up
- Racking Up Thousands of Dollars
- Have a Six-Figure Blogger Reveal the Truth
- Gain FREE Lifetime Access
- You Can Now Finally Start Living the Life You've Always Dreamed About
- Make Money from Millions of Online Markets
- "Profitlancing" to Their Success
- Fully Automatic Moneymakers
- "POURS" Cash Directly into Your Pocket Automatically
- Automatically Extracts Leads and Traffic
- Now Complete with a Revolutionary Breakthrough Technology

continued on next page...

...continued from previous page

- Discover a Lethal "Yet Ethical" Sales System
- Systematically Does the Selling for YOU
- You Can Actually Make Money on Google
- The "Street-Smart" Secrets
- Job-Ending Cash
- The Most Important True Story You Have Ever Read
- Powerful Yet So Easy
- Anyone Can Achieve Success
- Make Huge Sums of Money Online
- Only Once in Your Lifetime ... an Opportunity Presents Itself
- You Just Can't Pass It Up
- Sell the Dream
- I Cracked the Code and Discovered the Secret
- Now You Can Explode Your Income Faster and Easier Than Ever!
- Workhorse Methods Do Not Produce More Money
- A Complete Blueprint That Will Make Your Life Easier
- Skyrocket Your Income with a Speed You Never Dreamed
- All You Must Do Is Say "YES!"
- Grab That Opportunity Staring You in the Face
- Earn Your Living by Blogging Online
- You Can Make Money Online Quickly and Easily When the Path Is Cut for You
- It's True! You Can Dominate Your Market in No Time Flat
- Economy Down, Work Online Still Thriving
- It's Powerful and Easy to Apply

continued on next page...

...continued from previous page

- No Start-Up Cost
- No Experience Necessary

- Even Pro-Bloggers and Internet Marketing Gurus Are Raving About It
- I'm Letting Out All My Tricks, Methods, and Secrets!
- Discover How to Consistently Earn Between $___ and $___ per Day
- Quit Spinning Your Wheels
- Are You Ready to Learn the Secrets of Six-Figure Players?
- Finally Get Things Done!
- Are You Sick and Tired of Worrying About Money?
- Solve Your Money Problems Forever
- 98% of the Work Already Done for You
- Make Big Money Working Three-Four Hours a Day from Home
- Make Passive, Automatic Income Online
- Quit Going to Bed Feeling Guilty You Wasted Your Day
- Turn Twitter into Your Own Personal ATM
- I'll Give You This Automatic Moneymaker within Seven Minutes!
- STOP: Before You Buy Another EBook or Moneymaking System
- You Need This Information
- Build Your Own Google Fortune
- Change Your Life Forever
- Revealed: The Hidden Ace Up Google's Sleeve
- Reel in a Second Income from Home

continued on next page...

...continued from previous page

- Discover the Hidden Secret That Guru Super Affiliates Are Using Right Now
- Effortlessly Create MULTIPLE Income Streams
- Affiliate Review Sites Are Amazingly Powerful Cash Generators!
- Recruit an Army of Devoted Fans
- Create an Unstoppable Brand Presence
- Rake in Massive Commissions
- Become the Expert Before Your Competitors Do!
- You'll Rake in Unstoppable Commissions Easily
- Affiliate Marketing Is Your License to Print Money on Demand Anytime You Want!
- Create an Internet Cash Machine That NEVER Stops Spitting Out Cash for You
- Build Your Super Affiliate Business from Scratch, the Right Way!
- Build Your Website While Putting Cash in Your Pocket
- Quick and Easy System Anyone Can Follow
- Start Earning Income Online Even if You Have Completely No Idea How to Start!
- The Good News Is It Can Be Done Even if You're an Absolute Beginner!
- Consistent Income Month After Month Is More Important Than Any "One-Shot" Success!
- Advanced Technology That Just Works

Anchor Content—Blog Post Type Product Launch

Once you've published your content to your marketing blog, you'll want to market that content across the big sites including YouTube, Facebook, and Google+, as well as Twitter and other platforms you have a presence on.

As you build and create a list, you will also want to mail subscribers to share your new content. Over time, as you publish more and more great value-added content, more and more people will subscribe to your various platforms. This will allow you to drive more traffic and leverage the subscriber bases you've built up over time, and your marketing will have synergy.

We'll talk about how to do this more in the coming pages.

Your Marketing Blog: The Target

In the last few chapters, I've guided you through the mechanics of setting up an optimized WordPress marketing blog.

I shared the types of plugins you'll want to use, and I've covered not only how to add value but *tremendous value*. Once you've posted those first handful of anchor posts, you will have created the "traffic target," or the place you mention when people ask, "Where can I learn more about your ideas?" and you'll respond "At my blog." Ultimately, you will have created an asset that you can leverage again and again and that you can further add to over time.

✔ RECAP:

- Aim to launch your marketing blog with three to four anchor posts. Anytime you publish you should have two goals: to add value and to optimize your content for the search engines.
- Learn to say yes to opportunity instead of no. Example: You may not want to create videos where you're in the video itself; however, you can still leverage the platform to drive traffic.
- Make use of the 12-Step Trust Funnel Ranking Formula, and include various calls to action any time you publish something to the Web. Long-tail keyword phrases will drive traffic that is easier to convert into an action.

✍ HOMEWORK

- Launch your blog once you have written three or four anchor posts.
- Share your experience-based solution whenever possible.
- Leverage long-tail keyword phrases.
- Publish with users and the Google search engine in mind.
- Do not overanalyze or try to perfect your SEO when publishing; focus instead on adding value in that what you publish.
- Make use of the 12-Step Trust Funnel Ranking Formula.

CHAPTER 10

VALUE-ADDED PROMOTIONS AND THE AUTO LIST BUILDER

Let's take a moment to see how far you've come. By now you have laid a good foundation and are ready to build that all important *list*. You're about to turn those anchor posts into a hardworking sales force—one that will never ask for a day off, never need a break, and will continue to build another asset for your business: your list.

Even better, once the initial setup is complete, you won't have to spend any additional maintenance time. As long as your site is online and traffic flows, your list will increase on a daily basis.

Also note that what I'm about to share with you is *proven and based on my personal experience* with my own marketing blog. I increased my list-building conversions by more than fifteen times in one afternoon by simply tweaking the configuration of my site. Also, many other highly successful marketers have leveraged similar strategies, all focused around building that list!

After I spent four or five hours testing various conversion tactics, that number increased to an average of sixteen new subscribers daily. Furthermore, as I market new content on my blog, my traffic continues to increase as do the numbers on my subscriber list.

One of the focus items I'm working on as I write this book is to build my list via my own Trust Funnel; it's incredibly powerful as it's based solely on my actions and is not dependent on anyone else.

Thus, my list grows each and every day without:

- Product launches
- Joint-venture partners

Having a responsive list is an asset you'll want to nurture and grow. Your list, just like your marketing blog, will become the foundation of your business, and here's some more good news for you: This won't require much *additional effort on your part.* You won't need to create and publish additional content; rather, you'll simply share anchor posts that you've already published to your blog. Smart.

YOUR MARKETING BLOG IS ABOUT TO BECOME AN AUTO-LIST-BUILDING MACHINE

In the coming pages, I share the exact steps I took to set up my own auto list builder, and I'll also give you several options regarding list management, what to add to your site, and how. Before we jump into the how, though, I want to share some ideas concerning the list you will build and how to maximize the profits your future list produces.

If you've been in the Internet marketing space for any length of time, you most likely have heard the phrase:

"The money is in the list."

This is a half-truth. While building an email list will almost certainly improve your ability to generate income online, the money is really derived from the *value you bring to your list.*

Yep, here we are yet again, talking about adding value. It's almost beginning to sound a bit like a theme, wouldn't you say?

I know lots of marketers who have lists much larger than mine, yet I make far more income than they do. The money is NOT in the list; rather, the money is in the value you bring to those on your list.

Think about that. Your earnings are in direct proportion to the value you add to those people who subscribe not only to your list but to your Facebook page, your YouTube channel, and any of the other subscription-based Web properties you control. This chapter is about building and monetizing a mailing list. However, understand that all of those big sites are subscription based, and many of the philosophies and strategies I'll cover here apply to them as well.

I learned this golden nugget concerning "adding value" from Frank Kern, the self-proclaimed president of Internet marketing (inside joke), and it really stuck with me. I can remember watching a video where Frank explains the power of "adding value" to your subscribers. His wisdom is spot-on.

Here's another nugget I've learned over the years.

> *When you mail …*
> When you mail your list, you'll either be annoying or adding value.

It's really that simple. Every time you mail your list, you want to add value in some way. If you simply promote product after product and add little value along the way, you will annoy people and they will *stop opening up your emails* (disastrous for a marketer).

For this reason, it's important to focus on a *number of metrics* that are very important and will equate to how much (or how little) you earn with your mailing list. Of course, list size is important, and by adding value to that list, you can supercharge your earnings, as a higher percentage of people on your list will pay attention and act on your emails.

Here are the two fundamentals to focus on:

- Increasing your list size and consistently adding new subscribers
- Adding value to those on your list

Lastly, about "annoying folks" on your list, understand that at a certain point you will have enough people on your list that no matter what you do, some people will be annoyed with your actions.

After all, this is simply a numbers game, and when the numbers get big enough, sooner or later someone will lash out at you for something you do. It could be for promoting a product or emailing too often or even sharing FREE value-added content on your site. Expect this very thing. We live in a world of all different types of people; some of them are crazy and very well might end up on your list. It's important to prepare yourself and have a thick skin. Understand that even with the best intentions, you'll never please everyone.

TWEAKING THE MACHINE TO OPTIMIZE CONVERSIONS

Little changes and tweaks you make to a website can dramatically impact results, for better or for worse, and when you get it right, it's absolutely amazing what can happen.

Example:

Imagine you had a website that drove one hundred new visitors a day, day in, day out, like clockwork. No matter what you did or did not do, one hundred new visitors would access your site.

Now let's pretend (because pretending and dreaming are important to your success) that this particular website sold something (it could be anything: a book, software, whatever) for $100 and the conversion rate was 1 percent, meaning one out of every hundred visitors would buy. Thus, each and every day your little website would generate $100. Not too bad.

However, what if you could improve the site conversion from 1 percent to 3 percent with an afternoon's work? Think about that. You spend three or four hours changing various elements of the site, and instead of generating $100 from those one hundred visitors you generate $300.

BOOM! BAM! Ka-ching!

This is the power of increased conversions, and anytime you include a call to action you can test and tweak to improve on the results you're able to achieve.

I'm going to walk you through the steps and tweaks I made to improve the number of people that were signing up to my mailing list from my marketing blog. I mentioned "optimizing a call to action" in the previous chapter, and we're about to dig in deep.

Google Analytics For Website Tracking

By tracking the visitors to my website with Google Analytics, I've been able to track many factors to my site including visitor count, which pages are most popular, time spent on my site and more. You can do the same by signing up with Google Analytics or similar.

Now, back to optimizing the call to action. Note that the traffic to my site at the time was fairly consistent. However, I was able to go from one or two new subscribers a day to ten or twenty. That is a MASSIVE increase to one's list! And those are people I can connect with again and again and yet again. Let's look at the growth of my mailing list over the last six months based on fifteen new subscribers daily.

👍 **List Growth Based on 15 Newly Added Subscribers Daily**
Month One: 450 subscribers
Month Two: 900 subscribers
Month Three: 1,350 subscribers
Month Four: 1,800 subscribers
Month Five: 2,250 subscribers
Month Six: 2,700 subscribers

Here's the Same Breakdown for 1.5 Newly Added Subscribers Daily
Month One: 1.5
Month Two: 3
Month Three 4.5
Month Four: 6
Month Five: 7.5
Month Six: 9

Would you rather have twenty-seven hundred new subscribers that you can email anytime you like, or nine? This is the power of increased conversions and an optimized call to action.

WHAT'S THE VALUE OF A SUBSCRIBER?

This has been the topic of discussion in Internet marketing circles for many, many years. A popular response I've heard again and again is that for each person on your list you can expect to earn a dollar per month. I think this is a fair general assessment with the addition of the word *active*: You can expect to earn a dollar per month for each *active* subscriber that's added to your list.

Over time, some of the people that subscribe to your list may no longer use the same email address they signed up with, many will no longer be interested in the subject matter you cover, and some may stop opening and reading your emails.

I'll cover how to improve that last issue as we move forward.

However, just know that over time, the percentage of active subscribers (people who open and read your emails) will begin to drop. This is why it's so important to continue adding new subscribers on a daily basis and to ensure you're adding value so subscribers keep reading your messages.

Actual earnings will depend on many factors, including the email promotions you send, product price points, the number of times you promote various products in a given month, and how responsive your list is to you.

Bottom line is that highly successful marketers are all building a list, and you should too!

Derek Halpern of SocialTriggers.com is a whiz at psychology and what motivates people to take action online. On his blog and YouTube channel, he addressed the common question concerning list building: *"Derek, should I be building my email list?"*

His response: *"If you're not building your email list, you're an idiot."*

Strong opinion, for sure; however, here are some compelling facts that Derek mentioned.

While it's true that many people may get hundreds of emails per day, they're faced with thousands of Facebook and Twitter updates all vying for attention. The Web today is a very, very noisy place, and email will greatly improve the odds of getting someone's attention—much better than Facebook, Twitter, and Google+.

Furthermore, email gives you the chance to build a relationship with someone. It gives you the opportunity to demonstrate that you can provide a solution, and chances are that's what they'll be looking for in the first place.

Email is the bridge you can use over and over to connect with folks. It will lead to purchase after purchase; it's the core of your Trust Funnel. I hope you get how powerful building a list is. Now let's explore how I was able to increase my daily subscribers by such a large percentage.

BANNER BLINDNESS

I grew my subscriber list simply by addressing what's known as "banner blindness" and human nature. Generally speaking, people hate being sold to. They shut down and put up defenses when they encounter advertisements.

And for this reason, when a website visitor sees an advertising element (banner ad or list-building opt-in form) they often *consciously or subconsciously ignore* the advertising information.

Also, banners are all sized the same. The most traditional banner is 468x60 pixels and stands out on a website like a sore thumb, screaming, "Hey … I'm an ad, and I'm sized just like all the other ads you've been ignoring for years and years!"

Here is an example of a traditional 468x60 pixel banner:

468 x 60

COMMON WEBSITE STRUCTURES AND THE PATTERN INTERRUPT

Most websites have common structural elements including header, footer, and sidebar(s), and most webmasters fill in these various areas with the same type of content.

Header

This area contains the website logo, site name, and often a tagline or slogan. Other elements can include banner images as well as social sharing icons.

Footer

Typical use of this space includes links to privacy policies, disclaimers, contact pages as well as banners ads and social icons.

Sidebars

Sidebars almost always contain several elements including website navigation and banner ads as well as opt-in forms. In fact, chances are you'll find an opt-in form on most sidebars in nearly all digital marketing websites (focused on selling digital goods). And because this is so very typical, people ignore them (banner blindness). I have one installed on my site to track the signup rate of visitors to my site—the numbers are depressing.

Content Section

As you would think, this is the section of a website that features the content of the site, and it's also where visitors *focus their attention*. It makes sense, right? After all, visitors to a site are looking for a solution, such as the site owner's insight or perspective on a topic, and all of these items are found in the content.

Not in the header or footer or sidebar, but in the content section.

Pattern Interrupt for the Win!

Thus, instead of including your opt-in form in the sidebar, which is ignored by more than 99 percent of site visitors, why not include it right in the middle of the section that has visitors' full attention: the content section.

In the online marketing world, this is known as a pattern interrupt, and when I made these changes the results were dramatic. Install your opt-in form in the sidebar and get typical 1 percent conversion rates, or …

Install your opt-in form (and for best results, include a video like I did) in the content section and improve your conversion rates dramatically. I did just this back in early June 2013. Months later, I have added thousands of new subscribers that I would not have otherwise. Best of all, it only took me several hours to make the changes needed. Oftentimes it's not how hard you work but rather how smart you work.

The process of making this happen was simple:

1. I filmed a video talking about the exact subject of a post or multiple posts on my site. In the video, I mentioned getting access to additional free training, and I verbally told people to opt-in and pointed downwards.

2. Step two was to create a simple opt-in form using AWeber. Nothing fancy, just a simple AWeber form to collect email addresses. I then added the AWeber code to my blog post right below the video.

Tip: Over time you will likely have multiple articles that discuss similar topics. In my case, my marketing blog covers:

- Kindle self-publishing
- WordPress
- SEO
- Affiliate marketing

So the video I created spoke about Kindle self-publishing and accessing free information. I then used that same video and opt-in code on a handful of blog posts that were already published to my site.

I saved the YouTube embed code as well as the AWeber code on a text file and then added that entire string of code to the various posts that covered Kindle self-publishing. As soon as the changes were made, my subscriber rate began to increase right away.

This is exactly how I recommend you format your marketing site as well. There are several places to incorporate your call to action, including:

- In the middle of the blog post
- At the end of the article

It's not necessary to add video with a verbal call to action in the video itself, but doing so results in a much stronger call to action than simply incorporating text on a page. Lastly, I want to reiterate the importance of *telling the visitor what you want them to do.*

- "Add your name and email and click the submit button."
- "Click the 'add to cart button' and access this powerful training now."

You get the idea.

STEP-BY-STEP INSTRUCTIONS—
THE OPTIMIZED CALL TO ACTION

Getting Signed Up with an Auto-Responder Service

To build your own mailing list you will need to sign up with a commercial email service (also known as an auto-responder) that makes it possible to email to a list of thousands of people who have given you permission to do so. I personally use AWeber and have also just signed up with GetResponse. Many other marketers that I respect also use SendReach.

All of these services offer you the ability to create various lists as well as opt-in forms that easily allow anyone to add themselves to your list. These opt-in forms are what you'll incorporate into your various anchor posts with a call to action ("simply add your name and email address below") to build your list.

While all of these services are subscription based, they are critical to building up a business online. Do not be penny wise and pound foolish. Building a list is critical.

Create an Email "Follow-Up Series"

Once you have created the list, you'll want to add several email messages that are sent out automatically over a predetermined time that you can configure. This is known as an email series. I usually will create an email series of anywhere from two to four emails that link to additional free training available on my marketing blog or sometimes a product site.

Steps to Take:

1. **Create a list (most auto-responder companies allow you to have multiple lists).**

2. **Create a series of short follow-up emails**

   A follow-up email is automatically sent to anyone who signs up to your email list based on a preconfigured time schedule you determine. As soon as they sign up, they are sent message number one. Then, based on a timeframe you determine, they're sent a second message and so on.

   You can easily configure your follow-up email series to send your subscribers short introductions to your anchor posts on your blog. This way you don't have to create additional content right away. Later you can also create and add other follow-up emails that link to videos you upload to YouTube or additional blog posts that you create. Note that the first emails in your follow-up series should not be promotional; simply share the value-added anchor posts you created on your blog. This will make it easy for those who sign up to your list to get to know you and the content you share and ultimately trust you as they receive your first few follow-up emails.

After you have created and configured several follow-up emails, the next step is to create the opt-in form that will allow people to add their name and email address to your newly created list.

Create and Add an Opt-In Form to Your Blog Posts and Pages

All of the recommended auto-responder services offer tutorials on creating opt-in forms, lists, campaigns, and much more. You may want to access these tutorials for detailed instructions.

In your opt-in form, you will have the ability to add a bit of text; use this area to tell the visitor why they should sign up. Such as …

"Access the Passive Money Formula"

Then include the call to action yet again:

"Enter Your Name and Email"

Remember, if you decide to create a video, you can create one general "call to action video" on a topic that you will cover multiple times on your blog. Then you can use that video multiple times to add a strong call to action to your posts and pages.

Once you have created your opt-in form, you will want to save the code to a text file and then grab the embed code from the "call to action video" that you uploaded to YouTube. Insert this code from your opt-in form as well as the YouTube embed code into your blog post. Do this by using the text option in the WordPress editor after the entire post has been created.

You can access a detailed video tutorial on this subject here.

MarketingEasyStreet.com/optimized-cta

YouTube Embed Code

In the upcoming chapter about video marketing and YouTube, I will provide further details on how to leverage YouTube for traffic and more.

Value-Added Product Promotion—Blog and Email Marketing

With an opt-in form and call to action on your various blog posts and pages, your subscriber rate will start to increase as you market your blog content and more traffic flows to your site. In coming chapters, we'll cover how to drive traffic and thus gain attention and build up your list.

Once your subscriber rates increase, you'll be able to mail your list anytime you publish new content, and in essence you'll begin to drive your own traffic. And of course you'll also be able to leverage that list and your blog by including value-added promotions. Note that it's very possible to promote products and add value along the way. This is where a sustained business model comes into play, and here's why: If you're able to promote a product and add value to your readers, regardless of their decision to buy anything, then everyone wins—those that buy, those that do not, and of course, you! This is one of the paramount topics we'll explore in this chapter—how to add value as you're promoting various products and building your business.

Leveraging Email Broadcasts

In addition to series emails that are automatically mailed out to subscribers, you can also send out "broadcast" emails to those on your list anytime you like.

As we move forward I'll share how you can leverage broadcast emails to drive subscribers to affiliate promotions and ultimately cash in. In the last few pages

I've talked about why it's important to include different calls to action on your blog posts, with the varied goals including adding a comment, liking or sharing a page, signing up to a newsletter, or buying a product.

The same philosophy can and should be applied to your mailing list. That is, sometimes you might simply send out an email (broadcast or series) about a new blog post you just published covering a method or strategy that anyone can use to get a desired result.

This is a great example of adding value, and anyone who opens your email and clicks over to your blog will clearly understand that you're looking out for them and adding value. Thus, when you do promote a product or service, your subscribers will be more likely to open up your emails and listen to what you have to say. Promote a product or service that you see value in; you can do it in a way that offers value for everyone on your list and blog, *regardless of their decision to buy.*

In fact, let me go off the cuff and mention that I use this tactic often in webinar presentations. The philosophy is exactly the same. As the webinar is getting underway, the first thing I do is mention the following.

"Hey, it's Brian G. Johnson. First off, I want you to know that I absolutely value you being here. I know you have many options when it comes to webinars and how you spend your time. With that I want to let you know I'm going to do everything in my power to ensure that your time is well spent and that by the end of this webinar you will have lots of actionable tactics and strategies you can implement to take your business to the next level.

Regardless of your decision to buy anything with me here today."

This is almost like a reverse call to action. I'm letting them know upfront that I appreciate them spending time with me and they will get something out of that time, whether spending money or not.

So how do you do that with an email promotion?
Well, it's really not that hard. First you need to know the following:

- What does the product do?
- How can this benefit your subscribers?
- What are the positive factors concerning the product?
- What are the product's shortcomings?

Note that what I'll share in the coming pages works for all niche markets. However, I'll share some real-life examples with you based on my previous marketing efforts in the Internet marketing niche.

Funny, as I began writing this, a promotion from seven or eight years ago jumped into my head, one in which I was able to add value for everyone. At the time, I had focused my marketing efforts on eBay and was creating websites based around certain products on eBay including scrapbooking supplies, costumes, motorcycle trailers, used textbooks, and more.

Early on I populated my websites with traditional eBay affiliate ads that were keyword driven, and they successfully drove sales and generated great income. I began to share my ideas about eBay and how to get results with their affiliate program.

Then I created a website configuration based on auto-updating RSS feeds that were keyword targeted. This configuration was very powerful as Google was able to read and index the content that was pulled in via the eBay affiliate feed. Thus, my sites were updating hourly without me doing anything. This is good for SEO.

I began to share the strategy and people loved it! However, configuration was a bit complex—that is, until a new WordPress plugin made the setup simple and easy.

In my email promotions I was able to:

- Share with my readers the power of including eBay affiliate RSS feeds and the benefits they offered.
- Share my success (proof is powerful).
- Include details on how it could be done manually (a benefit for everyone regardless of a purchase).
- Share the plugin with my readers and the benefits of usage (simple and easy).

When you begin to craft email promotions in this manner, everyone is a winner, people keep opening your emails, and sooner or later a huge percentage of folks will buy. I have seen this happen time and time again.

Side Note: When they do buy, ensure you're adding value once again. If you're selling your own product, the process is simple. Assess other similar-priced products in your market and do better. If similar products offer several PDF files, then offer PDFs and video tutorials. If other products offer PDFs and video, then make sure your product offers those as well and include some live coaching sessions. If you're promoting an affiliate product, then add in a bonus item for your buyers.

I have personally followed this model for years; it works and has allowed me to generate a sizable six-figure income year after year. In fact, marketing online has allowed me to generate well over a million dollars in profit. Best of all, I get to live according to my own rules.

This method can be used in a variety of ways to reflect the importance of the product offering and ultimately how much time and energy you want to put into the promotion. You may run across a product that you're able to promote via the affiliate model, get excited about what the product offers, and quickly create an email based on those important factors. Once again …

Critical Product Elements to Cover:
- What the product does
- Benefits users will gain by using the product
- Product positives
- Product negatives

Larger Sale Multi-day Promotion

On the other hand, you may learn about an upcoming product offering or "launch" by an industry peer that you like and respect. You know the product will be a great fit for many of your subscribers (this is the most important factor; always ask yourself *is this good for those on my list?*).

In this case, you can create a series of emails and/or blog posts (super-smart tactic: send them two detailed blog posts about a product, and oftentimes your blog will rank for the product name, resulting in additional sales that you otherwise would not have generated). These emails can share some of the strategies, topics, or concepts that will be covered in the upcoming product—strategies that everyone on your list can benefit from, regardless of a purchase. Then with each new email or blog post, begin to reveal and highlight the product, point out the benefits to the buyer, what you like and don't like in the product, etc. And if you really want to drive sales …

Include a bonus for buyers.

Affiliate Promotion Case Study: AK Elite by Brad Callen

In May 2013, Brad Callen contacted me concerning a new Kindle software product he would be releasing that summer. At this point I was already very focused on Kindle and shared many of my list strategies and tactics. I had also released my first Kindle product in the late fall of 2012.

Aidan Booth, my partner at the time, talked about whether a promotion for Callen's software made sense. We both agreed that it was a great fit for our subscribers and my Kindle buyers, and we moved forward with our promotion strategy.

In July, Callen's software product launched, and from the get-go Aidan and I led the charge and won various contests including a prelaunch contest as well as generating the most sales for the product itself.

Please email me at ███████████ to let me know if you want the prize or the cash. If you want the cash, please send me your Paypal username.

On to the final AK Elite Leaderboard!

1. Brian Johnson & Aidan Booth (Maui vacation or $7,000 cash!)

2. Peter Garety (60" Samsung TV or $2,000 cash)

3. Jeremy Gislason & Simon Hodgkinson (Also wins 60" Samsung TV or $2,000 cash)

4. Eric Holmlund (Bose Soundlink Bluetooth speaker II or $500 cash)

5. Matt Callen (17 piece stainless steel cookware set or $250 cash)

Our cash prize alone was $7,000, and we also generated more than $10,000 in affiliate commissions. Most important, everybody won. Those who did not buy were able to access some cutting-edge strategies that Aidan and I blogged about and emailed to our list. We promoted the prelaunch, which again included access to an in-depth Kindle guide that anyone could get for free.

Tip: In the Internet marketing space, most prelaunches are based on a free giveaway that anyone can obtain simply by signing up with their email address. Thus, if you promote a prelaunch, many of your subscribers will opt-in and you will be building the business of those individuals—and you may or may not get paid.

Many Internet marketers will not promote prelaunches for this reason. However, on the flipside, understand that many of your subscribers *may* learn about the launch and prelaunch regardless, and some will opt-in. And by sharing good information that adds value, you can naturally lead your subscribers into a sale in a very ethical manner.

Remember, great results come from building trust, adding exceptional value, and sharing both the good and bad points of any product you may want to promote. A well-organized prelaunch and subsequent launch follows this format very nicely. For this reason, Aidan and I decided it was a good idea to promote, and in the end it helped our promotion.

EMAIL PROMOTIONS AND LARGE PRODUCT LAUNCHES STRATEGY

Single Product Focus

In the Internet marketing space, the number of products launched on a daily basis is staggering. This can and does confuse people as to what tools, courses, software apps, and coaching programs they should be purchasing.

Case in point: Have you ever been at the grocery store standing in the ice cream aisle wondering what flavor to choose? Heck, I have paced back and forth for several minutes for a darn tub of ice cream that will cost me a couple of bucks.

It's a proven fact that when people are faced with *multiple decisions* (more than three) they often **do nothing**. Not surprisingly, the most popular ice cream flavor is vanilla. The decision to purchase vanilla is simple. Everyone enjoys vanilla. The decision is an easy one.

Thus, instead of promoting different products day after day, why not go *all in on one product* that you really believe in? Doing so makes the act of purchasing easier for your subscribers, just like buying vanilla ice cream!

This strategy benefits your subscribers because you're not confusing them; plus it builds trust.

It can also put you in the limelight with industry peers and ultimately result in more cash in your pocket by continuing to drive sales for *one single product* rather than multiple products. This can result in additional earnings thanks to product launch cash and prizes. Lastly, this strategy can put you on product launch leaderboards (demonstrating your ability to get results).

Planning: Know What You Will Promote Prior

Any product promotion you do will benefit greatly from planning, and there are a number of ways to plan out your promotional calendar. In the Internet marketing space, several sites are dedicated to product launches.

Thus you can simply access these sites from time to time to learn about pending launches. Of course, you can also network with other marketers in your niche. You will often get a heads-up email from those who are launching.

Put it on your calendar! It will make your life so much easier. When a new product launch is happening that I feel is a good fit for my list, I block out a good chunk of time. Of course, how much time I put toward a promotion depends not only on the product fit and my subscriber base, but the price point and commission payout as well.

Higher price points and joint venture cash and prizes also determine how much effort I will put in. This is a business, and I need to pay the bills just as much as I need to bring good products to my list.

You can find several Internet marketing calendar sites below:

MarketingEasyStreet.com/internet-marketing-launches

Planning the Promotion Out

The following steps are based on what I typically do for a large-scale product launch, and it always begins with planning out the actions you will take that include:

- Coming up with a bonus for buyers
- Thinking through emails that will be sent and when
- Creating a bonus page that outlines the product and my bonus offer

Give yourself enough time to do what's needed, and you will be less stressed and able to create an awesome bonus webpage.

Creating a Bonus and Bonus Webpage

First things first; when the product launches, you'll want to give potential buyers incentives to ensure that they *purchase with your affiliate link*. This is actually easier than you might think. By simply including your own bonus item for any buyer, you will increase your sales dramatically. This is especially true in the Internet marketing world. Many marketers include a bonus, and for this reason. No surprise then that many buyers of Internet marketing product will search out the best bonus for a product.

You will want to promote your bonus HARD. Let your subscribers know that it's the best bonus for product xyz and here's why. This is a great example of playing your hand. If your product is just one item, mention that the last thing a buyer needs is dozens and dozens of bonus items. Instead, all they need is one truly valuable bonus that is based on the product itself.

What do you offer buyers? Lots of stuff! I prefer to create my bonus items myself; this way the *only* place anyone can access my bonus is when they buy with me. Below I have included a list of ways to create a special bonus package.

Exclusive Live Group Training Based on the Product

Offer buyers an exclusive training live with you. You can use any webinar platform including Google Hangouts, which is free. During the exclusive live event, go over the product, best practices, and any other idea, strategy, tip, or tactic you might want to leverage that's focused around the product.

Also, mention in the bonus page that this will only be available to buyers and that you'll also personally address anyone on the live event during a Q&A session.

Exclusive Personal One-on-One Training Based on the Product

If the product is priced high, you may want to offer personal one-on-one training via Skype or Google Hangouts. Offer email support as well. By far, this is one of the most sought after items when it comes to the Internet marketing niche. People want help and guidance and are often unsure. Thus, offering personal access can get results. Remember the golden rule: Find out what people want, and give it to them.

Exclusive Personal Video Training Based on the Product

This is an excellent bonus strategy and is pretty easy to facilitate. Simply create one or more videos focused around the product. The video could be a product demo, best practices, or strategy based.

Exclusive Personal Report or Case Study Based on the Subject Matter
You might also want to create a report or case study based on the video materials you create. This way, if people like to read, you're giving them what they want once again.

Exclusive Interview, Training, or Overview with the Product Creator
Ask the product creator if they're open to an interview which you can record and offer as a bonus. You will find that many product creators are open to this. You can record a Skype call or create a Google Hangout to facilitate this.

Exclusive Access to Your Upcoming or Previously Released Product(s)
If you're working on a product that you will launch in the coming weeks, you can offer your buyers access. This is a great bonus offer as your offer will have a price tag associated with it in the near future. If people have been following you and getting value from your blog, many of them will want your product as well.

Access to Product Bundle: Software, Reports, Audio, Video Training ...
All of the above examples are based on items you would have created, and in my experience they are more valuable than something that was not created by you. However, sometimes you will not be able to create items yourself. In this case, you can still offer a bonus package to buyers by leveraging PLR (private label right) materials or by accessing a bonus from the product creator.

Many PLR products are available for you to buy and offer as a bonus, and in doing so you will be sweetening the deal for your buyers. When buying PLR, your goal should be to focus on the product at hand and to create a bonus package that is based on the same or a similar topic. Thus, if I were to promote a product on video marketing, my bonus would also be based on video marketing and/or YouTube. Also note that you can use a PLR product as a starting point in the creation of your own exclusive bonus.

Example: You buy a PLR report on leveraging YouTube and then create five videos based on the materials in the PLR report.

Bundle Any of the Above Examples into Your Super Bonus Package
The more *real* value you can add with a bonus the better. I personally do not add bonus after bonus simply to show a "huge pile of stuff." However, depending on

the product price point, commission structure, and possible JV cash prizes, you may want to include several items as listed above into one super bonus.

If you're thinking that this seems like more work, you are correct. It takes a bit more time and energy to put together a bonus package. However, by thinking of an affiliate promotion more like your own product launch, and by including an extra bonus, you can earn *tremendous amounts of money* while also *adding tremendous value* for your buyers.

Since 2008, this is the exact strategy I have used on large-sale product launches, and thus I've been able to generate five-figure paydays again and again. Lastly, what I'm sharing here is an example of going all out, and it makes sense when you can generate a sizable payday.

Sometimes I may simply send an email because I believe in the product and figure many of my subscribers would want to know about it. No bonus, no big promotion, just a simple email.

Once you have figured out what your bonus will include, you'll want to publish a *bonus web page*—the sooner the better. This way Google has a chance to index the page, and that can result in more traffic from people seeking out reviews and/or bonus packages prior to buying.

This is very powerful on a number of levels:

- You'll make more money from people NOT on your list; they end up finding you because you targeted the product name + bonus and/or review.
- These buyers that are not subscribers never would have heard of you until this point; thus you have a chance to demonstrate that you have what they want: life experience and possible solutions to something that's important to them. They may buy from you again in the future. Again, it's all about adding tremendous value.
- You'll earn recognition from industry peers as someone who can drive results.

You can launch this page on your own marketing blog, or you can launch a standalone website targeting the product name + bonus or review. This is exactly the strategy Aidan Booth and I took in the summer of 2013. The result was a number one Google listing for the term: **AK Elite Bonus.** As mentioned earlier, we won the JV contest, drove a lot of sales, and earned a bunch of cash money—awesome.

Simply follow the 12-Step Trust Funnel Ranking Formula when creating your bonus page or site. If you plan to purchase a domain based on the product name, *check with the product vendor* to ensure that's okay. In the Internet marketing space, most vendors will not care. However, you'll still want to do the polite thing and ask.

If you go the route of a product name domain, I suggest ONLY going with a .com. Over the last several years, I have noticed that the .com keyword target domains continue to rank very well for product name keyword phrases. Other extensions do not have the same ranking power.

When it comes to the bonus page offer, you'll want to focus on *your* bonus first. Below I have included two example sites that each generated five figures in affiliate commissions as well as cash and prizes. Notice that with each example bonus page below, the focus is on the bonus offer.

Example Bonus Page #1 AK Elite
AKElitebonus.com

This bonus page is short, sweet, and right to the point: "Our bonus is the best. Check it out."

In this example, the bonus package was created using the strategies and tactics mentioned above. Our bonus was comprised of an older product that was still very valid, software products from the actual vendor, and several brand-new items created specifically for the bonus offer.

We spent about twenty minutes figuring out what we would use as a bonus and then created the actual bonus page. Notice that the title begins with the target keyword phrase: AK Elite Bonus.

Once the visitor landed on the page, they got a sneak peek at the actual software bundle as well as an overview of our bonus. This is known as a bonus stack. The idea is to stack the value for the buy and highlight that on the actual page.

This simple bonus stack offer works very well. Below you can see the sales generated from our offer.

Example Bonus Page #2 Authority Hybrid

Just as with the example above, this next bonus page focused specifically on my bonus offer, which was coaching. Instead of listing the exact bonus items first, I focused on how powerful coaching can be and presented visitors with a simple question.

• • • • • • • • • • • •

A Coach or Mentor ...

The Karate Kid, Luke Skywalker, Rocky Balboa and Brett Favre
All Had One ...

So Did a Skinny Kid from New Zealand Named Aidan Booth Who Has
Quickly Dominated the Internet Marketing Space in a Matter of Years.

What's Your Plan?

• • • • • • • • • • • •

I included a video of me sharing details about coaching and my bonus and kept the focus on that question in the headline: **What's Your Plan?**

Marketingeasystreet.com/authority-hybrid

This particular bonus page was published to my marketing blog and also ranked very well in Google for my target long-tail phrase: **Authority Hybrid Bonus**

Pro Blogging, Make Money Adsense - My-Affiliate-Program...

Toward the end of the page I focused heavily on my bonus and once again earned substantial commissions of five figures.

Once your bonus page is published, you can move forward with other tasks.

Prelaunch

Prelaunch often happens several days to a week prior to a launch, and as mentioned, it usually kicks off with some type of giveaway. If I have time, I will create a blog post several days prior to the start of prelaunch focusing on a similar topic or strategy as the topic for the giveaway. This way I am educating my subscribers and piquing their interest in the subject of the prelaunch materials. This step is not necessary but does align their attention to the upcoming promotion, and it also adds value.

Prelaunch — The Giveaway

Next in sequence are the prelaunch emails. The goal is simple: to get as many people to sign up as possible (also known as opting in to the prelaunch sequence). It's important to understand that anyone who signs up will also be marketed to when the actual paid product goes live, and those individuals will be tagged with your affiliate ad.

A great angle to use during any prelaunch that features FREE content is just that! Simply mention that there is some tremendous software, an ebook, or a WordPress plugin that's very good and worth people's attention.

I often like to begin such an email like this:

It's rare that you can find such great content for free. However, today that's exactly what you get right now.

Mention what's in it for them. Go through the materials and bullet point several key factors that folks should pay attention to. I also mention that this content is part of a product launch and that there will be a paid product available. I may end with, "The content is awesome, and you don't want to miss this!"

This way you're upfront with your subscribers and letting them know there will be a paid product promotion coming as well. People like honesty, and this will speak to your integrity.

For one week before prelaunch, I usually email my list twice. This will always increase the number of people who opt-in to the free offer and promotion.

Just Prior to the Actual Product Launch

About a day or so prior to the actual paid product going live, I will again email my list and cover those critical product elements I mentioned earlier, both positive and negative factors. I also mention *any bonus* I will be offering buyers of this product.

Then I link to my already published bonus page. This gives subscribers a chance to check out the bonus package.

Email Subject Lines

For this email subject line I **mention the product name** (by now, anyone who has opted in to the freebie info will most likely know the product name) and the word **BONUS**. This gives all subscribers a heads-up that if they indeed buy the product using my affiliate link they will get an extra bonus item that is only available from me. This locks in sales and ensures that people will use my affiliate link.

Product Launch Is Now Live!

As soon as the paid product goes live, email your subscribers once again with a subject line that mentions the product name and your awesome bonus.

It's critical that you email them as soon as *the product goes live*. With all the emails you sent up to this point, many folks are going to be very interested and will want to buy. As soon as the cart opens up, they will do just that.

Direct them once again to use your special affiliate link, letting them know that by doing so they are eligible for your awesome bonus package.

The Day After the Launch

I almost always mail again on the second day of the paid product launch. This will drive additional traffic and sales. Lead off with the benefits the product offers and why you're excited about the product. Of course, you should once again mention your bonus and link to your blog post featuring the bonus offer.

Time to Change It Up! Lead with Your Bonus Email

At this point in the promotion, many of the people on your list have already decided they will purchase the product, and some will have already done so.

So instead of sending out additional emails with the product name in the subject line, I change up the promotion and begin to sell my bonus hard—focusing entirely on the bonus package (in the subject line).

This often results in additional sales, as folks are buying access to your bonus offer. An offer I've used with my list has focused on personal one-on-one coaching. This is something I rarely offer, so it makes my bonus offer appealing to those on my list.

Last Chance—Closing Down Soon

Fact: During a large product launch, the most sales will happen on day one of the promotion, and the day the launch closes down will generate the second best sales in a single day.

I have seen this time and time again in my own product launches, and I hear similar results from other vendors. Thus, you'll want to email at least once during the final hours of any launch.

In the case of Brad Callen's launch, my partner and I were about fifteen sales away from increasing our joint venture prize by $5,000, and we had already emailed a ton. However, we emailed out again, mentioning that it was the "last chance" for our bonus and access to the product at a discounted price—and generated enough sales to hit our target.

Moral of the story: Even after emailing a fair amount, you can often still drive additional sales when an offer is closing down. Scarcity is a powerful motivator. People do not like to lose out on a deal or special offer.

A WORD ABOUT PROMOTING HARD

As I wrote this section of *Trust Funnel*, I realized that many people may think it's unethical to promote so hard, to email people repeatedly and encourage them to buy. I thought this way for many years and sometimes still struggle a bit with it myself.

Finding the place of adding value and selling can be tricky; however it's important to remember a few things. Most important of all is that you get behind and push for a product you believe in—either your own product or a product by a vendor you trust and respect.

The people on my list are often looking for guidance; they want to be pointed in the direction that can help lead them to success, and by offering a bonus item I created just for the product, I'm again adding value.

There's nothing wrong with selling when it's done in an ethical and responsible manner. Sure, by this point in my career—with thousands of people on my list—some of them will *not* like what they read. Or they will think of me in a negative light because I am selling. But thousands of people do find my information helpful, and many of them have earned significant amounts of money based on what I publish.

No matter what your niche market is, never be afraid to sell and sell hard. The key is to ensure that you're adding value to your list along the way. Do that, and you will create a thriving business.

✔ RECAP:

- Don't question for a minute if you should build a list; the answer is yes.
- Focus on adding value when you email your list. Earnings from your list are based on several items, including list size, how responsive readers are to your emails, and the value you bring to the table.
- Sooner or later someone will call you out for something. Understand that as your list grows, someone will not be happy with your actions. Focus on the majority, and don't let the haters get to you!
- Banner blinds can dramatically impact results in a negative way, so use a website pattern interrupt to increase opt-ins to your list. During a promotion, focus on adding value to everyone who is reading, including buyers and non-buyers.
- Creating a bonus page can result in more traffic to your site and more buyers. Smart!

🖾 HOMEWORK

- Get an auto-responder account.
- Include optimized calls to action to build your list (video is especially effective).
- Plan out promotions and don't feel bad for promoting hard; focus on how you can add value for everyone who reads your emails.
- Creating a bonus offer page on your website can drive more traffic and increase earnings.

CHAPTER 11

VIDEO MARKETING AND THE POWER OF YOUTUBE

On July 6, 2007, I uploaded my first video to YouTube from my home in Minnesota. Technically, the video was terrible. The audio sounded like it was traveling through a tin can. The visual clarity was bad due to lack of lighting. This first video was a "welcome to my website" video in which I read from a script. For much of the shoot I did not look into the camera as I was reading—something you don't want to do!

🐾 Pro Blogging, Make Money Adsense - My-Affiliate-Program...

This video did not follow my golden rule of Internet marketing. I had yet to learn and understand it myself.

The video did not help to solve a problem or add value, and thus as I type this (March 2014) the video has received only 1,316 views, two thumbs up, and three thumbs down!

It was a flop and a failure.

In the coming days, however, I would publish video after video, many of which *did* add value, and so I began to build an early fanbase. Many of those fans would become not only customers but repeat, rabid customers I am still in contact with today.

These days, I'm much better at video than I was back in 2007. When I look at these early videos of mine the first thought I have is just how terrible they are. My immediate perception spans the whole gamut: The technical quality is terrible, the content is terrible, the delivery is terrible.

Remember that perception thing I mentioned in the previous pages. Well, the perception of those very first YouTube viewers had *nothing at all to do with failure.*

In early 2014, I posted a question to Facebook asking my friends (many of whom are customers) if they found me via my early (and terrible) YouTube videos. If so, I asked them to please post the approximate date of that discovery and what they thought of those early videos. The response I got, time and again, was that I was real, authentic, and helped them to move forward. What I want to bring to your attention is that the people who found me via YouTube were not looking for dazzling videos full of effects.

Rather, they were seeking out information, and they wanted authentic, personable, and timely solutions to their problems. You may also think that any video you create will not be good enough; however, if you focus on delivering your experience-based solutions, you will be following the golden rule and people will dig your videos.

Most people don't care about fancy cameras, professional lighting, or stunning visuals, just the content itself. Always focus on the content rather than the container. This was a phrase I heard from onetime partner Alex Goad. Brilliant stuff.

GIVE VALUE, FORGET THE TECH!

When it comes to leveraging video, we're going to focus on *easy* and *prioritizing our efforts, focusing on what's most important.* Do not get bogged down with technical details, because they simply are not needed to drive results.

And time and time again I have seen people struck by the power and potential of making supershiny, Hollywood-like videos end up making NOTHING. Why? Because they get in over their head with the tech, hit roadblock after roadblock, and eventually quit.

Once you stop, you fail.

Thus, we will not be blinded by the supershiny; we will focus on what others need and want, and we'll get it done! We will adhere to the golden rule, using video to create a closer bond with potential customers, subscribers, and web visitors, because that is what matters. No other form of media allows you to share your *experience-based solution* better than video.

👍 It is not necessary to understand any of the following to made value-added videos:

H.264
H.263
AVI
MPEG
MOV
Absorption loss
Alphanumeric
ASCII
Attenuator

I'm not saying you shouldn't want to learn some of the technical details, but rather that you should focus your efforts on traffic, conversions, and building assets.

Thus, as we move forward, I'll provide you a roadmap that will make creating game-changing videos online simple and easy (really). If you already use video but are not happy with your current results, I urge you to take inventory of what you're doing day to day, how you're spending your time, and modify your workflow to produce more video based on the *needs* and *wants* of those in your market.

GETTING FANCY IS FINE
(ONCE YOU'RE PROFICIENT WITH BASICS)

As you progress with video, understand that you can and should want to learn more that will help you to improve your video quality overall. However, just know that the focus should remain on the content, not the container.

WHY YOUTUBE?

Why should you use YouTube and not one of the other video services? The most important component of the success you desire is traffic, and no other video site can match the number of viewers that are on YouTube each and every day.

The three most popular websites on the planet are:

- Google
- Facebook
- YouTube

When it comes time to post your videos online, don't you think it makes sense to go with the most popular video site, the very one that so many of your potential audience is already using? If you're still not convinced, check out this impressive list.

- **#1 Video Site:**
  When it comes to Google listings, YouTube videos are found more often than other video services.
- **#2 Search Engine:**
  YouTube is the second largest search engine on the planet. Bigger than Bing, Amazon, and others.
- **Mobile Simplicity:**
  YouTube makes video easy, plain, and simple. Upload a video and YouTube will optimize every video stream for each individual user to watch based on device, Internet connection, location, and more.
- **Quality HD Playback:**
  YouTube is capable of playing incredible HD-quality video. Upload a great high-definition video, and it will look great for your audience.
- **Easy and Free Embed Player:**

YouTube makes the process of getting video from YouTube to your website simple, and you won't pay a cent for hosting of the video files or streaming.

- **Google+ and Google Hangouts**

  YouTube is tightly integrated with Google+ as well as Google Hangouts, both of which allow you to leverage live video that others can attend. Want to host a live streaming event? Google Hangouts makes it possible and can greatly push rankings, views, and subscribers for your YouTube channel. Furthermore, videos from your YouTube channel can be featured and shared across your Google+ page and account. Yet another way to tap into a massive audience, some of which will most likely be interested in your niche market.

- **Ability to Scale Traffic via Google AdWords**

  Yet another powerful reason based on the most important success element—traffic. Any video publisher can easily leverage the Google AdWords advertising platform to serve inexpensive ads to a huge audience. Even better, those ads can be targeted to a specific audience in a number of ways. So when you publish videos to YouTube, you can take advantage of advertising options if and when you like.

SETTING UP YOUR YOUTUBE CHANNEL

Sign up for your account and you will notice a myriad of options, settings, and buttons to click. You could spend hours and hours fiddling around with these various settings and not get very far with the primary goal.

Remember: Focus on the creation of assets based on the golden rule of Internet marketing: *Find out what people want, and give it to them.*

Yes, you should spend a bit of time setting up your channel, but focus on the most important aspects of a YouTube channel that people will want to return to. This includes uploading channel art designed around your brand, creating YouTube playlists that focus on specific types of videos, and creating a trailer video to welcome people to your channel.

Connecting Your YouTube Channel to Google+

Earlier, when you created the Gmail account to secure your social profiles and brand address (URL), you automatically created a Google+ account and a YouTube account that are now automatically linked together.

This is helpful and beneficial as your Google+ account profile page can display recent YouTube videos that you have uploaded. Having linked accounts also allows deeper integration with Google+ and paves the way for you to host live Google Hangouts which are then saved to your YouTube account. I discuss some of these benefits as we move on.

Custom Channel Graphics and Branding Elements

Today all the big social sites allow you to customize the look and feel of your channel, and YouTube is no different. There are two key graphical elements that you will want to upload and include to brand your YouTube channel effectively: your *channel icon* and *channel art*.

Channel Icon

The channel is a small, square icon that is not only attached to your YouTube account but also your Google+ account. For this reason, it can show up in a number of locations across YouTube, Google+, and in the Google search engines:

1) Next to any videos you upload.
2) Next to any comments you make on YouTube.
3) Next to any comments you make on Google+.
4) Possibly in the Google search results if you set up Google Authorship.

The channel icon should be a headshot of you, and anyone who knows of you should be able to recognize your icon/photo. As mentioned, this image will go a long way in establishing your trust and authority over time.

The channel icon should be a square graphic, 800x800 pixels in size. The image will be reduced in size; however, the higher the resolution you use the better (in terms of image quality). This is not a place where you want to try to incorporate text; it's far too small. Instead, focus on using a photo that people will begin to recognize over time.

Channel Art — Larger Cover Image

While the channel icon is rather small and provides little space to get creative, the channel art is plenty large enough to do just that and you should! As mentioned earlier, your best bet is to hire one designer to create all the graphical elements you'll need across all the social sites, including YouTube.

The dimensions for the channel art are 2560x1440 pixels. However, they may have changed as you read this. The good news is that by hiring someone who focuses on this type of work, they will know exactly what is needed.

YouTube Channel Art

Channel Art Option—Gallery

If you are not able to hire a graphics designer, or you want to set up your channel before getting your branded graphics, you can use some preset cover art options that YouTube has provided. This is better than not adding anything. You'll find a gallery of channel art options by clicking on the header portion of your channel and selecting "channel art."

Channel Links

YouTube makes it easy for you to connect your channel to your other social media profiles as well as your marketing blog. To do this, visit your channel homepage while logged in and hover over the channel art. You'll see an option to edit your "channel links." Again, these options may have changed slightly by the time you read this. If you're not able to locate where to do this, try a Google search.

Make sure to connect all your social profiles here; it will allow future fans to find you across multiple social sites.

Featured Channels

YouTube gives you the option of linking out to other channels if you so desire. This can be useful if you have other channels online (such as me) and want to point people in the direction of your various channels.

Another option is to link out to a channel you feel is providing great content that your users can benefit from. Think outside the box! Perhaps you can find another YouTuber who would also be willing to feature your channel in the same manner.

Channel Trailer

This is a great feature that allows you to create a custom "call to action" video that will only be shown to visitors who have not already subscribed to your channel. This video should be short, clear, to the point, and provide visitors with a "subscribe now" call to action.

Note: This is a video you will not want to change often if at all. As more and more people view the video, the view count will go up creating social proof for you. Again, be sure to be very clear in your message.

- Make use of several "subscribe" calls to action:
  - an audible call to action when you tell them to subscribe
  - a visual call to action that displays "subscribe" wordage
- Tell them why they should subscribe and what's in it for them.
- Share your personality.
- Be short, clear, and to the point.

Tip: When uploading your channel trailer, you have an option to make the video public, private, or unlisted. Select unlisted; this way, current subscribers won't see that video.

YouTube Playlists

After you have had a chance to upload a number of videos, YouTube makes it possible to group similar videos together to form a playlist. To do this, access your channel homepage and click on the link "playlists," and YouTube will walk you through the process.

This is a great way to make it easy for visitors to find videos on a certain subject. For example, since I have been teaching Kindle for the last few years, I've gone ahead and created a Kindle playlist. This way, anyone who finds my channel that is interested in leveraging Kindle can view a Kindle playlist.

Channel Layout Options

YouTube allows you to customize your channel layout in a number of ways. You can add popular videos, recent videos, liked videos, playlists, upcoming events (Hangouts), as well as completed events.

The goal is to highlight your best videos, playlists, and events on your channel homepage. To begin customizing your channel, access your channel page while logged in and click on the channel name area of the site. Here you will be given a chance to modify that area.

The Videos—Most Important Element
Found in a Great YouTube Channel

Everything you've done to this point is intended to highlight the most important element of your channel: the video content itself. You can have the greatest channel art, channel trailer, and branding elements in place. However, if the actual content within your videos does not add value, you will struggle to get the results you're after.

Thus, your primary focus should be to create videos based on the wants and needs of your potential audience. In the coming pages I'll share some supereasy video creation methods you can leverage to create videos that add value—using cameras, screen-capture software, and even $2.99 video apps I've used with much success.

Learn One Video Creation Method First

Anytime you're learning a new skill set, strive to make the process *as simple as possible*. When you were young and learned to ride a bike, chances are you learned with training wheels. When someone begins to train to run a marathon, they don't venture out and run twenty miles on their first outing.

It's much easier to learn a new skill one step at a time. Thus, when you begin to learn how to create videos, don't worry about fancy transitions, adding titles, incorporating whiz-bang effects, or catchy audio.

Rather, focus on the content and keep things as simple as possible. I've done this for years, and it makes the complexity of Internet marketing a bit more manageable. As I learn various crafts, I add on new tasks and challenges, and my skill set grows. Let's take a look at several video creation methods you can use with much success.

You in Front of a Camera Talking, Sharing, and Demonstrating

Just as it sounds, this method involves you standing, sitting, or demonstrating a task in front of a video camera (or smartphone). This method is very easy, does not require fancy equipment, and can be used to share ideas verbally, to demonstrate a task, and more. I personally have used iPhones as well as mid-grade HD camcorders (Canon HG10 and HG20) with success.

If you have a spare bedroom, office, or den, you can easily create a simple makeshift video studio with a tripod and microphone hookup. Nearly everyone I have taught or spoken with was nervous when creating their first few videos. To this day, I sometimes get a bit nervous. That's okay. It simply means you care.

However, I encourage you to push past that fear, as these types of videos are easy to create and greatly benefit your business.

Screen-Capture Video—Another Great Option

Chances are you've probably seen screen-capture videos before. Screen-capture video can be used in a number of ways to create various types of videos including sales videos, tutorial videos, "how-to" videos, and more.

Several software products on the market allow you to create these types of videos including Camtasia, ScreenFlow (for Macs) as well as CamStudio, which is available online and free.

I've used Camtasia myself for years; it can be used to capture PowerPoint or keynote presentations (great for sales videos) as well as live screen-capture video. Highly recommended.

There's an App for That!

Can you believe there's an app for iPad that makes it possible to create pretty darn good videos for a whopping $2.99? It's called Doodlecast Pro and lets you create presentation-style videos via the iPad. With this app, you can import images from your saved photos, draw over those photos, and speak at the same time, similar to a PowerPoint or keynote presentation. The app records everything, and uploading to YouTube is a snap. I've even used this app for promoting a $500 product and sold a ton!

GENERAL TIPS FOR VIDEO SUCCESS

Get to the point and pronto. Honestly, this is one that I'm working on myself. That is, to get to the point as soon as possible. I don't think there is any rule on how long a video should be. However, most people start to lose interest after a very short period of time.

The largest YouTube ranking factor is based on how long people watch a certain video. If viewers leave within seconds of a video starting, chances are that YouTube will not rank that video well. However, if the majority of those who watch actually view till the end, that sends a strong message to YouTube that people like the video. YouTube will likely push that video up the rankings in its search engine.

Priority: Lighting and Audio

So many people who are getting started with video focus on the camcorder or camera. However, the greatest way to improve the overall quality of a video is to *ensure good lighting*. This can be done in a number of ways, and you don't have to spend an arm and a leg on equipment.

Over the last few months I have been filming videos with my iPhone with no professional lighting. I have a spacious room in my home that faces north, and the room is filled with lots of bright indirect light … perfect. The quality of these videos is absolutely fine and a great example of doing the best possible job without getting carried away with professional lighting, expensive gear, and complexity.

I'm not saying you shouldn't use professional gear; just know that you can create awesome videos that address the needs and wants of your viewers without it. If you're not able to find a well- lighted room, you might want to invest in some inexpensive lights. A quick search on Amazon for video lighting kits will return plenty of options for you.

Shooting Video and Pictures Outside

Shooting outside can often result in great-looking videos as well as still images due to the natural light, when you're aware of the direction of the sun. Always have the subject facing the sun or in the general direction of the sun. The camera person should have their back to the sun. Simply being aware of the direction of the sunlight can make a huge difference in your shots.

Quality Audio

Quality audio is another area you'll want to invest in. I've mentioned "not to get hung up" on technical issues, and you certainly don't want to do that. However, if you get serious about video, doing what you can to improve the audio will benefit you and your audience, and the process is as simple as plugging in a better microphone. By having a lapel microphone, you will greatly improve the overall sound quality. I use a special microphone adaptor for my iPhone that I pair with a wireless lapel mic, and the quality of the audio is splendid.

For The Superserious! The Dedicated Video Room Setup

Want to focus on video and need to get set up with the right gear? If so, don't break the bank on the camcorder alone. Instead focus on these four items and you will be able to shoot some amazing videos for your marketing blog and YouTube.

- Camera
- Lighting
- Microphone
- Tripod

It's very possible to pick up a great HD camcorder, a two-point video lighting kit, and tripod for less than a thousand dollars. In fact, I'll be moving into a new home soon and plan to create a dedicated video room using these four items myself. While it is very possible *not* to invest in a lot of equipment, doing so allows you to more easily control your video recording environment.

Video Editing

There are a number of suitable editing programs on the market. I've personally used Pinnacle Studio and iMovie with success. Having used both a PC and a Mac for video editing, I prefer a Mac and find iMovie plenty powerful.

When you're first getting started with editing, keep it simple and understand that you will learn a great deal as you edit more and more video. MP4 is the industry standard format for exporting videos online. Always export the largest and highest quality videos possible. This will improve the audio and video clarity and overall user experience. Also note that YouTube will scale down your videos based on each user's location, Internet connection speed, and other details. All you need to do is render a high-quality video and upload. YouTube will optimize for you.

Video Titles and the Call to Action

All video editing programs allow the editor to add what are called titles (not to be confused with the words you use to "title" a video as you upload it to YouTube). A video's title is a playable part of the video itself and often is used to introduce the video and to add a *call to action* at the end. Titles are usually comprised of a few words of text, a solid background color, and/or simple graphical elements. You'll absolutely want to make use of titles for your videos.

The Intro Title

Make sure to include a few simple words describing what the viewer will get by watching your video. Also include your domain name or anything else you may want to bring to people's attention, including any product or service you may be promoting.

Some of the intro titles I've used for videos have included my domain name and ebook cover art (social proof and positioning).

Intro Title Examples:

Note: By including the graphical cover of my ebook into the intro slide, I am positioning myself as an expert in self-publishing while also drawing attention to the ebook itself, which could generate additional sales.

The Ending Title

At the end of any video you create, you'll want to include some type of call to action. This could include:

- "Visit my website at: YourDomain.com."
- "Visit Amazon and grab your copy of my latest ebook."
- Asking people to leave you a comment.
- Asking people to share or like the video.

The ending call to action should be both visual and verbal. As you say, "Visit my website at: YourDomain.com," the ending title should reflect the same call-to-action message.

Examples of Ending Call-to-Action Titles:

(Go to MarketingEasyStreet.com for more awesome.)

HOW TO RANK ON YOUTUBE AND GET MORE VIDEO VIEWS

Just as the Google search engine ranks webpages, YouTube ranks videos based on the keyword phrases you'll use when uploading your videos. Note that this does not mean easy video rankings simply lie in choosing the correct keywords to incorporate into your video titles, descriptions, and/or tags. *They do not.*

However, you will want to carefully target long-tail keywords that people are searching for and incorporate them into your titles, descriptions, and tags as seen in the image below.

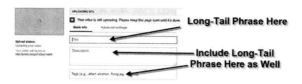

Rather, rankings are based on length of average view time as mentioned above. Thus, you'll want to go out of your way to focus and deliver on the golden rule. The more value you bring to your video, the longer people are likely to watch and engage in the video itself. This is what will push your video to the top of the YouTube rankings and allow you to drive more traffic back to your site, build a bigger list, gain exposure, and more.

Ensure that you're creating your YouTube video titles based on long-tail keyword phrases. Begin your title with the long-tail phrase and also include it several times in the description as well as the video tags.

Target Keyword Phrase—Title Tag

Simply begin the title with the long-tail phrase you want to target. You may also want to include additional single keyword phrases you discover while researching potential keywords. Do not create a title longer than sixty-five characters as Google will only display the first sixty-five or so characters.

Target Keyword Phrase—Description Tag

The first thing you'll want to add to the description of your video is a link to your site. If you've created the video specifically for a blog post, then link to that specific post. Otherwise simply link to your homepage.

Make sure to use the full address beginning with "http" as shown in the example screen capture above. After the link, I like to start my description with my target long-tail phrase and a colon. Then I add a paragraph of text that describes what my video is all about.

Target Keyword Phrase—Tags

Tags are single words or short phrases that further describe what your video is about. I usually add around a dozen or so tags to each video I upload. The process is simple, and there is no need to overanalyze tags. Just add words and phrases that describe what your video is about, and you're golden.

More Tips on Tags

I do have one tag tip for you and that is to add the same one or two tags to each video you upload. This way YouTube will often group your videos together and recommend more of your videos to viewers who are already watching one of them.

A great tag to use is your domain name; for instance, I always add the tags:

- marketingeasystreet.com
- briangjohnson

Understand that as you add more and more videos and more people watch and engage with your videos, your channel will become a more powerful marketing platform.

Custom Video Thumbnails

A video thumbnail is the graphic that is overlaid on your video and displayed on any webpage before the video begins to play. This includes YouTube, the Google search engine, and any website that embeds your video.

Think of the video thumbnail as a little banner advertisement. A great video thumbnail can improve the number of views by enticing people to click and watch. Thumbnails are generated automatically when you upload a video; they are still shots taken from the video itself. However, you can also create a custom video thumbnail that gives you much more control.

How to Create a Video Thumbnail

In order to use custom video thumbnails, you'll need to have a verified YouTube account. A verified account lets YouTube and Google know that you're a real person in order to reduce Web spam.

When signing up for a YouTube account, you may have been asked to provide a phone number. This allows YouTube to send you a message via voice or SMS that contains a small code. Enter this special code to verify your account, and you'll be able to take advantage of advanced YouTube features such as custom video thumbnails. If your account is not verified and in good standing, simply search YouTube or Google for "verify my YouTube account" and access corresponding pages found on Google and/or YouTube.

Creating and Uploading the Custom Thumbnail

Thumbnails should be designed for 16:9 aspect ratio. I like to create thumbnails based on a resolution of 1280x720. YouTube will automatically resize as needed, and the higher the resolution, the greater the quality of the thumbnail image.

YouTube supports the following image formats: JPG, GIF, BMP, and PNG. Note that the image must be smaller than 2 MB in size.

Canva.com—A Great Free Online Tool for Graphic Creation

Earlier, I mentioned spending a few bucks to hire a professional photographer. If you do hire one, think about having some shots taken where you're pointing up or to the right or left. This way you can use these images to create great social media memes as well as custom thumbnails and lots more. Once you get the pictures back, you'll be amazed at how many ways you can use them!

Canva is an online image creation site that makes the process of creating great memes and social media-type images a snap. You can leverage predesigned graphics, color schemes, sizes, and shapes. You can also upload your own images, which makes it possible to easily create eye-catching custom thumbnails.

- Access Canva.com.
- Select a custom size and enter 1280x720.
- Upload a photo you want to use.
- Make sure to resize, scale, or crop the image so there is a lot of blank space to work with. This is where you will enter a few words of text.
- Enter in the desired text as needed. Focus on the keywords you targeted.
- Select the largest size possible for the text. Remember, the image will be greatly reduced in size, and you want people to be able to read the wording.
- Select a font and color and then save.
- Upload on the "upload video" page, and you're set.

To Upload or Edit a Video on YouTube
- Access the YouTube video manager.
- Locate the video you want to edit, and click the edit button.
- Click on "thumbnail," and upload the desired image.

Example of Regular YouTube Thumbnails

Example of Custom YouTube Thumbnails

Notice in the second screen capture I have included a cover of my Kindle ebook in the thumbnail; this gives me added exposure for my ebook and brands me as an expert in self-publishing.

Also note that the video targets the terms "Kindle Countdown Deal and Promotion," and the words on the thumbnail are exactly that: "Kindle Countdown Deal." This lets the Web surfer know that my video is about Kindle Countdown Deals and promotions.

STACKING THE DECK AND LEVERAGING YOUTUBE

One of the things I love about YouTube video marketing is that each video you upload can be leveraged in a number of ways. Most obvious is that YouTube visitors can find your videos, and that may result in more traffic to your website and more exposure for you and your brand. Second, YouTube makes it very easy to transfer your videos from YouTube to your website.

Furthermore, the videos actually stream from and are saved to YouTube, so you don't need an expensive hosting account. YouTube will manage it for you. To add any video to your site, simply visit the page where visitors would find your video, click the share button, and then click on "embed." This will display a special YouTube code that you can add into your blog post. You'll want to add this code via the post or page editor using "text mode."

Lastly, not only can you add your video to your own website, but if you make your video public when uploading, anyone can access the embed code and install your video to their website—more exposure!

Note: A handful of plugins and themes allow additional functionality when it comes to embedding YouTube videos.

TYPES OF VIDEO YOU MAY WANT TO CREATE

1) **Interview Style**

   Simply put, you interview someone or they interview you using one of several video platforms, some of which include Google Hangouts, Skype video calls, or FaceTime. This can be incredibly powerful as you can leverage the authority and expertise of someone else or yourself.

2) **In Front of the Camera**

   This can be done quickly, easily, and alone with no need for help from others. I use this method myself and have driven hundreds of thousands of video views. Wicked.

3) **Screen-Capture Tutorial (great for technical teaching)**

   Various software programs allow you to easily "video capture" what's happening on your screen. This can be used to demonstrate how to do technical things online such as create a Facebook ad, upload a video on YouTube, or format a Kindle ebook. A must for anyone in the Internet marketing niche.

4) **Story-Based "Lesson Learned"**

   These are deeply personal-type videos where it's all about you sharing an outcome, either positive or negative. In summer 2010, I lost my AdSense account, which had generated close to $150,000 at the time and was on track to make 75K that year. Sharing this truth with the world via a video was scary, but it allowed me to share a "lesson learned" with my audience—in the hope of ensuring this same fate did not happen to them.

5) **News or "Just In"**

   This is an update video where you're sharing industry news. An example would be shooting a video at a conference and going into detail about a particular presentation and/or something that happened at the event that others in your niche market would find interesting.

6) **Welcome**

   Simply stated, this is a video that welcomes new or returning visitors to your marketing blog, social site, etc.

7) **Product Review and Affiliate Offer**

An in-depth product review can add a lot of value for people. This is especially true when adding in your own bonus item for buyers.

If you're looking for specific instructions on getting signed up as an affiliate with various companies, you can find numerous tutorial videos on YouTube covering the specifics. However, let's stick to the overall strategies here. Let me state that the review must be authentic and reveal both the positive and negative aspects of the product. Anytime you're asking for money, you need to over-deliver to drive the most sales.

This means:

- Truly reviewing the product and showing usage (if at all possible).
- Providing your own recommendation as to why this is a good product and why someone would want to buy it.
- Focusing on the benefits buyers will experience with the product.
- Your review and bonus offer should be, in part, based on the value the product will bring to buyers as well as the cost.
- Demonstrating how you'll be using the product yourself.

Combining Various Video Content Creation Methods

To separate your content from the competition, why not combine these various types of videos into one longer video and/or several individual videos posted to one anchor post?

Example: Happy New Year's—WordPress SEO Tutorial Video Series

In that anchor post, I incorporated the following three video types:

- Welcome introduction video
- Tutorial video
- Product review

I welcomed folks to my page, offered numerous tutorial videos on the subject at hand, and also incorporated a "soft sell" of a product (OptimizePress 2) that resulted in a few hundred dollars. Note that the goal was not to sell anything but rather to deliver value to my readers and get links from other sites, as well as social media shares and likes. Thus, to make several hundred dollars on top of that was icing on the cake.

✔ **RECAP:**

- **Video for Trust, Traffic, and Conversions**
  Video is an incredibly powerful platform, and with today's smartphones and point-and-shoot camcorders, the process of creating video is easier than ever, and one I highly recommend you look into.

- **Smartphones and YouTube Make It Easy**
  Shooting a great-looking video that can be quickly uploaded to YouTube, Facebook or other social sites is straight forward if you keep things simple.

- **An External Microphone and Lighting**
  The easiest and most effective way to increase the overall quality of the video you create is to simply be aware of the lighting and audio when shooting. An external microphone is a great way to improve the quality with no technical know-how needed.

- **Uploading Video Success**
  Remember to include keyword phrases in both the video title and description that users would search for when looking for videos similar to what you're publishing.

HOMEWORK

Take the time to think about the various types of videos you want to incorporate into your marketing blog, knowing that videos are a powerful media type that can not only drive traffic but convert more of that traffic into an action such as signing up to a list, buying a product, or sharing content with others.

In the next chapter, were going to look at another one of the "big sites" that not only can drive considerable traffic to your marketing blog, but will also pay you month in and month out. I'm talking about Amazon.

CHAPTER 12

AMAZON KINDLE: INSTANT AUTHORITY, TRAFFIC, AND EARNINGS

They told me to remove it. That is, my publisher told me that this very book, *Trust Funnel*, was far too many words, contained too many images and that this would all result in too many pages.

And this would hurt overall sales.

For this reason they told me to either remove a chapter or two or that they would not be able to publish my book. However, I simply was unwilling to completely remove any chapter. They were all important to the overall scope and vision for this project. However, I wanted the backing of a big publisher, one that could get *Trust Funnel* into more hands.

Thus, we agreed to remove this chapter from the physical book, but to make it available as a download. That way, you would not miss out on the power and profitably that Amazon and Kindle can provide.

. . . .

Download missing chapter twelve
and access additional training videos at:

TrustFunnelAcademy.com/missing

Instantly access chapter twelve by
entering your name and awesome email address.

. . . .

CHAPTER 13

LEVERAGING FACEBOOK AND OTHER SOCIAL SITES

n the fall of 2011, I created my battle plan for the coming year, which included leveraging traffic sources other than Google. My primary focus for 2012 would be Kindle; however, I also began to spend more time on Facebook.

I want to mention a few things before we jump into social media marketing, notably that I *concentrated my efforts on one social site* to start with, not four or five. This is always how I move into learning anything new. I like to focus on a few targets, and I don't move forward with the next "shiny new" opportunity until what I have been spending time with has become an asset to my business.

This is why I chose to focus only on Facebook in 2012. Today I have thousands of friends and followers on Facebook, and while numbers are a metric that can be used to measure your influence, a better way to gauge influence and your ability to leverage social media (to find customers, drive traffic, and ultimately make money) is *engagement*. In other words, how many people engage with you on Facebook, Twitter, Google+, or any other "social" site.

This should come as no surprise. I've already mentioned that establishing engagement is important with your marketing blog. Your goal should be to increase comments, shares, and likes—all of which are signs of strong engagement on your marketing blog and the social sites alike.

Thus, you're far better off having a thousand friends on Facebook, many of whom comment and engage when you post, than five thousand friends who rarely comment, like, or share. With that, understand that you should not chase more "friends" but rather that you should seek to build *relationships and engagement*.

In this chapter I want to share my personal experience with using Facebook to drive traffic to my website, build a list, and ultimately build my business. As with the last few chapters, I'm going to draw your attention to only the most important aspects of using social media to increase your overall business.

LEVERAGING SOCIAL MEDIA TO BUILD YOUR TRUST FUNNEL

In this book I've shared a quote from Zig Ziglar that had a massive impact on me and what would become *Trust Funnel*:

> *"If people like you they'll listen to you,*
> *but if they trust you they'll do business with you."*

Everything starts with getting attention, which can and often does lead to people liking you and in time, trusting you. Social media is a great place to grab that attention and get the "like" ball rolling. And each and every day, millions of people access social media sites; thus you'll want to be there too.

THE SOCIAL MEDIA PLAYBOOK

Let's talk a little bit about the rules of engagement—that is, how to get the most out of social media sites like Facebook, Twitter, and LinkedIn.

For the most part, people go to these sites to have fun, connect with friends, and share pictures of kittens and silly memes. Generally speaking, people do not head to Facebook to learn about specific things or to seek out advice as they often do with YouTube or Google. Thus, the marketing messages you post to social sites should reflect this.

Again, simply follow the golden rule: *Find out what people want, and give it to them.*

If they're there to have fun, make sure what you post reflects this. Your posts should also reflect your core brand. If you have a wacky sense of humor (as I do), then share that. If you are more analytical, then again, what you post should reflect that, but do it in a way that is engaging and accessible.

Earlier I mentioned Bill Nye the Science Guy. He does this very well. He makes learning science fun by sharing his own personal brand.

What NOT to Do

Earlier I mentioned that people love to buy but they hate being sold to. Do not post ad after ad with the hopes of driving a sale or opt-in. People will see this as exactly what it is—advertising—and will *tune you out*, rendering your ability to leverage social media nearly useless.

Instead, give the people what they want; share a variety of messages, and you will begin to capture a very rare commodity online—attention. In time, some of the people who follow you will begin to like your updates, and as you know, liking can and often does lead to trust. Thus, if you were to post an update from your blog about an affiliate promotion or live event, many more people would be interested in checking it out.

If you have yet to sign up for Facebook, I suggest that you do. Before moving on, let's talk about Facebook basics, what drives viral activity, and ultimately what powers the Facebook algorithm.

Just as with Google, an algorithm decides which status updates should get more visibility. Understanding how the algorithm works will help you to get more out of the time you spend on the world's most popular social site.

Basic Facebook Mechanics

Facebook is nothing more than a network of people who have agreed to connect with one another. A connection is made when one person sends a "friend request" to another Facebook member who approves the friend request.

For instance, let's say Bobby and Sue used to be friends in high school. Bobby signs up for Facebook, searches out Sue, and sends her a friend request. Sue accepts the request and the two become "friends" on Facebook. Now, anytime either Sue or Bobby updates their status, the other will *potentially* see the status update.

The Facebook Newsfeed

Anytime you post a status update or share a status update, it is added to the Facebook newsfeed of those people you're friends with. The average Facebook user has two hundred or so friends, and this is where things begin to get a bit tricky.

How does Facebook determine how visible your status updates are on your friends' newsfeeds? In other words, when someone logs into Facebook and accesses their personal newsfeed, which status updates are featured first? After all, if most people have two hundred friends, that's an awful lot of updates from hundreds of people—some of which may not be visible due to sheer volume.

Engagement is what Powers Facebook Visibility: Like, Comment, and Share

Not only do friends get updated to one another's statuses, but they can also *engage with one another* by commenting, liking, or sharing a status update. Click the little thumbs-up Facebook icon in someone's status update, and you just engaged with them by "liking" their update.

Engagement is the social currency that drives Facebook and determines just how visible status updates are. When a status update has a lot of engagement (likes, comments, and shares), Facebook will often push that update to the top of the newsfeeds. Let's take a deeper look at our example with Bobby and Sue. Not only are they Facebook friends, but let's say they each have two hundred friends on the social site.

While on vacation in Hawaii, Bobby updates his Facebook status with a picture of himself surfing. His friends love it! Most people like and comment on the photo, and as Sue logs into Facebook, the first status update she sees in her newsfeed is Bobby's surfing picture from Hawaii.

In contrast, if Bobby were to post an update that received very little engagement, Sue might not ever see it but rather would most likely see updates that had lots of engagement. This is the Facebook algorithm at work and it determines status update visibility.

Understand that this is a simple example and many other things determine which status updates gain visibility and which do not. Strive to *create updates that are engaging*. Make it easy for people to comment, and interact. Ask simple questions, share fun events and pictures. Typically, these are the type of status updates that draw more attention.

As a marketer, you can connect with more people by sharing a variety of messages and updates that over time will draw attention, likeability, and for some, trust. Once in a while you should post an affiliate promotion you're featuring on your marketing blog or an anchor post that you want to promote.

However, more often, simply sharing something fun will result in keeping your status updates visible. Thus, when you do share a promotion, more people will see it due to the fact that you're not simply spamming promo after promo (which would not engage people). Many newcomers to social media fail to learn this lesson and struggle.

PERSONAL PROFILES AND BUSINESS PAGES

Facebook and Google+ offer users the ability to create different types of properties on their sites including:

- Personal profiles
- Business profiles (also known as pages)

Generally speaking, you should increase the percentage of "business like" posts on a business page and share your personal stuff on your personal page. That being said, understand that many in your niche market may seek you out and want to connect on your personal profile (Facebook specifically) and that it's fine to share some business updates on the personal account. Later, I'll get into how many social media marketers manage both types of accounts.

Setting Up Your Personal Profile (Timeline)— Cover Image and Profile Image

Your personal profile page, also known as the Facebook timeline, can be modified with two images: the cover image, which is a larger image that runs across the top of your timeline, and a profile image that is smaller and located near the top left of the page.

The Cover Image

Here you might want to include a cool picture of the outdoors, a larger picture of you, perhaps a graphic, or whatever you like. Be creative and have fun. Note that you can change your cover image anytime you like. I change mine about once a month or so.

The Profile Image

This should be a picture of you. For best practices it should be a headshot that allows people to easily recognize you. You can tweak the profile image as you see fit; however, I strongly suggest that you keep a picture of yourself in this shot.

Profile Image   Cover Image

Since this is your *personal profile* page, you have a bit more liberty as to the kinds of images you use with both the cover and profile image. However, when you set up a *business page* your images should reflect your business brand.

I would recommend that you don't change these often. The idea is simple. This is where you share business tips, ideas, and content—it's all business.

You want people to easily recognize your profile image anytime they see it in the newsfeed. Furthermore, your business page should be branded in the same style as your marketing blog. It's all about congruency.

Changing these images on either your personal timeline or business page is easy. Simply access the page, hover your mouse over the image, and select "edit."

CREATING A FACEBOOK (BUSINESS) PAGE

On the top navigation bar you will see a drop-down arrow that provides various functions, including the creation of a page. Click the arrow and select "create page."

Next, you'll have a chance to name the page. I suggest you name it the same as your marketing blog, then select what kind of page you want to create. Some of the choices you will have include:

- Local business or place
- Artist, band, or public figure

- Company, organization, or institution
- Entertainment
- Brand or product
- Cause or community

Select "brand" and continue. Note that the name you select for your page can't be changed. Thus, you'll want to make sure the name of your page is exactly what you want. Next, you'll have a chance to upload your cover and profile images. Your profile image should be a headshot of you and your cover image should be branded to your website. That is, the images on your website (header and logo), should look very similar and be based on the same colors, font, and text size.

Now you'll want to fill in the "about" page information. Keep this short and to the point, a few sentences about you and your business. Include a link to your website. Lastly, add in some starter content that will welcome new visitors to your Facebook page.

Page Likes—The Gateway

Once a Facebook user likes your page, they will potentially see any future updates you post to that page. One thing that is so powerful about social media is that once someone likes you or a page, to a degree they are *subscribed to you* and your messages. In this book we've talked about just how profitable list building can be. Well, with Facebook, Google+, YouTube, and other social sites …

You are building a following of subscribers.

How often you post to your profile or business page is really up to you. However, I would suggest a minimum of two or three times weekly and no more than three or four times daily. Understand that Facebook status updates can be very simple photos or graphics with a simple message.

In fact, these types of posts, often called memes, do quite well.

Facebook users scroll by update after update. The medium is "short-attention-span theater," and this is why these types of updates do so well. The content is quick and easy for the end user to digest.

SO WHAT SHOULD I SHARE ON FACEBOOK?

On your personal profile page (timeline) remember that anything goes. Mix things up and have fun. What you're cooking for dinner, your latest vacation adventure, a book you're reading, and then, once in a while, feel free to post something that is more commercial.

A great way to do this:

First, post the commercial status update to your Facebook *business page*, then share that update on your personal page. This way, anyone who is friends with you on your personal page may also "like" your business page, allowing you to connect with them more often on a business level.

Again, the idea is to share with others and have fun!

Be Interesting, Be Memorable, and Grab Attention

Earlier, we spoke about creating your superhero storyline—about creating an avatar for your brand which is ultimately you. It's all about grabbing attention and keeping people interested.

But I'm an introvert! you say. Well, it's easier than you may think. Colin Theriot talks about being an introvert who has a difficult time approaching folks at conferences. However, he has created his own unique and interesting storyline, and *people approach him.* Colin mentions picking up a pair of bright green shoes as a way to stand out, and they also give people an easy icebreaker at events: "Hey, where did you get those crazy shoes?"

I ended up with a silly haircut that people kept mentioning time and time again. My haircut was their idea, not mine. I simply followed their lead and went with it.

Bill Nye the Science Guy wears a bowtie. It's these little things that can separate you from your peers or competitors. Sure, it takes guts to rock a silly pair of shoes or funny haircut. However, a bowtie certainly is not that scary.

Once you begin to define your brand, find your style, and "write" your storyline, the process gets easier and easier. Facebook, Google+, and other social sites allow you to fly that freak flag of yours, and I suggest you do.

SOCIAL MEDIA STATUS UPDATE IDEAS

Power Images
If you've spoken from the stage on the topic of your niche market, or if you've published a book or received some type of award based on performance within your niche, you'll want to post these images as well. I like to think of these as "power images" because they display your expertise within a niche market.

Sharing Other People's Updates
Share other people's status updates, and in turn some of those folks may very well share your updates. This gives you additional exposure you would not have had. Of course, when you share someone else's content with your audience, you're providing the exposure for them as well.

For this reason, lots of folks do not share, and that's a shame. If you put the needs and wants of your audience first and bring them great content, they will take care of you in return.

Business-Based Tutorial—Linking to Your YouTube Channel
Here's an example where I did in fact post something that was business related. I shared a tutorial video from my YouTube account, and it was very well received. Note that it was simply strong content with nothing to buy or opt-in to, and the feedback was great. This particular status update was shared five times. Not too slouchy.

Quotes from Famous People
Sharing great quotes is a simple and easy way to post updates that add value to people's lives. Even better, coming up with the content is as easy as doing a Google search or two. In this status post, I quoted Napoleon Hill and got some great engagement from my friends.

> **Brian G. Johnson**
> March 23 near Colorado Springs, CO
>
> "First comes thought; then organization of that thought, into ideas and plans; then transformation of those plans into reality.
>
> The beginning, as you will observe, is in your imagination."
>
> – Napoleon Hill
>
> Like · Comment · Promote · Share   2
>
> Jennifer Jackson Koenig, Ron Goilehon, Edward Moore and 25 others like this.

Facebook Makes Video Simple and Easy

If you have a smartphone and/or modern camcorder, uploading video to Facebook is a snap. There is no worry about video format or complexity. Instead of clicking on the "status update" link, choose "add photos/video," select the video you want to upload, and you're set.

I have uploaded serious as well as funny videos with much success. In the image below it was a cold, snowy day in late March. Folks on Facebook had been complaining about the "never-ending winter," so as the snowflakes began to fall, I ran outside and shot a silly "weather update" video and the response was tremendous—sixty-plus likes and thirty-five or so comments. I have also posted serious videos that were also well received. Again, when it comes to sharing on social media, variety is the key.

Advice I Ignored (Save Some of Your Best Content for Later)

As you can see, it's all about being creative and leveraging simple ideas and tools to create memorable status updates. When you have something that you know will go over well, and it's a biggie, plan it out and use it to your best advantage.

That being said, over the years so many people have given me the following advice that I never really took:

"Save your best for the next project."

~or~

"Don't release everything right away."

What I've learned over the years is this: If you do little, then of course coming up with great content is challenging. However, the more you do, the easier it becomes. This is especially true of the craft you will teach. For instance, when it comes to Internet marketing, the more chances I take and the more I publish …
the more ideas and content I have to share.

Building Relationships and Engaging with Others

Up to this point, the focus has been on you and what you will be publishing. However, one of the very best ways to supercharge your Facebook marketing is to seek out others that you want to work with and friend them. They could be possible partners as well as customers. Spend a few minutes a day seeking out others you may have worked with in the past or peers that you would like to form a business relationship with.

If you are just getting started in your niche market and are not sure who the players are that you should be engaging with on Facebook, simply search Google for your niche plus "guru," and you will most likely find one or two high-profile gurus that are already established within your niche. Then search for these gurus on Facebook and like any pages or profiles you may find.

As mentioned, once you like or follow any page or profile, you will see any status updates from these gurus, who often have a large following. Comment and engage with their status posts, and over time others may follow you as well. This is an old-school tactic that has worked for me and countless others time and time again. Also note that folks who comment and engage are extremely interested in the topic at hand and are the very kind of people you want in your network.

Fast Friends—Leverage That Email List

Also, make sure to let others know via email that you're looking to connect on Facebook and/or any social media site you're focused on. This is yet another way to leverage that email list and supercharge your marketing. Understand that over time, as your mail list and social property subscriber bases increase, you'll begin to pick up more and more synergy.

Program Your Facebook Account for Success

The good, the bad, and the ugly. There's plenty of it in the world today, and it's also found on Facebook and other social media sites. Once you've become friends with a handful of people and have liked several Facebook pages, your newsfeed will be filled with all kinds of messages that will impact you …

for better or for worse.

Let me go on record right now and say that Facebook is programming the minds of millions of people, and most have no clue. However, you are now in the loop and can program your newsfeed for success.

If you're told each and every day that you're a loser, sooner or later you'll start to believe it. By the same token, if you hear that you're smart, savvy, and fun to be with, in time this message will have a positive impact on your mental outlook and you will believe it as well.

Allow me to quote Jim Rohn:

"You are the average of the five people you spend the most time with."

When I was young, I participated in sports including track, cross-country, bike racing, cross-country ski racing, soccer, and many highly competitive games. I always strived to hang out and practice with those who were better than me. In doing so, my game improved in a massive way.

In soccer, I was able to kick more accurately; in bike racing, my average speed over dozens of miles increased, as did my ability to strategize. With time and practice, that allowed me to finish on the podium again and again.

Surround yourself with winners, and you too will become a winner. You can and should do this on Facebook. Over time you may find that you're friends with someone who generally brings you down in some way, shape, or form. And each time you see an update from them, these feelings may surface. If this is the case, then by "unfollowing" them you will no longer see messages from these people.

Let me mention that with Facebook, you can unfollow someone but still remain friends. Thus, why not program your newsfeed with positive messages, people, and status updates that can have a positive impact on you.

I did this very thing. I unsubscribed to various email lists, unfollowed people who brought me down, and sought out Facebook pages that published positive messages. The results have been tremendous, and I have no doubt whatsoever that it has contributed to my overall happiness and success.

Priorities, the Productivity Ritual, and Facebook

As an online entrepreneur, your day will be filled with many tasks: publishing blog posts; filming, editing, and uploading video; working with outsourcers; networking with peers; responding to comments on your blog; planning and preparation; and much more.

This is why prioritizing your efforts is so very important.

In the previous pages, I mentioned the power of the productivity ritual and how over just a few short weeks you can create a positive work habit that will allow you to focus your time and energy daily on what's most important.

In order to achieve a high level of success as an online entrepreneur, there are several things you must have:

- Value-added content that your market is able to obtain (both free and paid)
- Exposure, or traffic to your blog and any Web property you control
- Relationships that you nurture (customers as well as partners and peers)

Facebook is a powerful platform that will allow you to address all of these items. However, it is imperative that you publish value-added content that addresses the needs and wants of those in your niche market.

Also, let me qualify the term "value."

Making someone smile or laugh is adding value. Sharing a post from someone else that engages people is adding value. Don't think that "adding value" means you need to publish in-depth blog posts time and time again. You should focus on doing that some of the time, just as you should also share a fun picture of yourself at dinner with a friend, a silly selfie or similar. In the coming pages, I will cover various types of status updates that work well on Facebook.

A great place to start is your marketing blog where you have total control over what you publish and how. This allows you to publish free content that builds trust while also publishing and promoting paid content.

Everything starts with item number one. Thus, I'm going to suggest that you focus your productivity ritual around that very thing.

GOOGLE+ VERY SIMILAR WITH SEVERAL EXCEPTIONS

Google+ and Facebook have many similarities, and once you get the basics of Facebook down, you'll be able to jump in and leverage Google+ as well.

Spend a few hours setting up your Google+ account and you'll enjoy instant gratification when it comes to traffic generation, thanks to several benefits that only Google+ offers.

Google Authorship

This is a biggie, and we covered it in an earlier chapter. Simply add a Google Authorship plugin to your WordPress marketing blog and your Google+ profile picture may be included within the Google search engine listings as mentioned previously.

On average, Google Authorship makes up around 20 percent of Google listings, and having that image next to a listing builds trust and can greatly improve CTR (click-through ratio) and thus traffic.

Google+ Indexed by the Google Search Engine

The Google search engine crawls and indexes the Google+ network, and when a Google+ user is logged in, Google will often return Google+ listings that have been posted by Google+ users the searcher is following.

Did you get that part?

Here is an example of how this works day to day. I have thousands of Google+ followers, and one day I posted a status update to Google+ about how to drive "more Kindle book sales."

Today that post is indexed in the Google search engine, and any of my followers who search Google for such content may very well find my listing. Also, many SEO experts believe that Google+ passes PageRank. I personally do not think that is what people should focus on. However, if that is indeed the case, it's a positive thing.

THE #1 SOCIAL SIGNAL IN TERMS OF GOOGLE RANKINGS

What about the future of search engine marketing and SEO? How will social signals such as likes, shares, tweets, and Google+ impact Google rankings? This is an important question, and chances are strong that one day they may impact the rankings directly.

As of spring 2014, Google has mentioned (and often) that social signals do not "directly" impact rankings. However, I personally believe that may very well change. After all, social signals are based on human activity, and what better way to gauge rankings than by polling the very people who are interested in the subject at hand.

Some SEO experts speculate that we're already there and that social rankings do directly impact Google rankings, and that Google +1s carry the most weight. On August 20, 2013, The Moz blog posted an article about the incredibly strong correlation of Google+ and high Google rankings, citing that Google+ was the second strongest factor overall.

"Every two years, Moz runs a scientific correlation study to discover the qualities of web pages that have a strong association with ranking highly in Google. This year, for the first time, Dr. Matt Peters and the Moz Data Science Team measured the correlation between Google +1s and higher rankings.

The results were surprising.

After Page Authority, a URL's number of Google +1s is more highly correlated with search rankings than any other factor. In fact, the correlation of Google +1s beat out other well known metrics including linking root domains, Facebook shares, and even keyword usage."

source: moz.com/blog/google-plus-correlations

Do Google +1s impact rankings?

It's really hard to know; however, they do carry so much goodness that can translate into rankings and targeted traffic, that you'd be foolish not to leverage the Google+ network.

The rules are about the same.

Understand that Google+ is a social network and that you should post a variety of status updates. When you publish a value-added anchor post, by all means post a status update to Google and link to your anchor post. This can drive additional traffic, encourage social sharing, increase social proof, and lots more.

GOOGLE+ SECOND LARGEST USER BASE OF ACTIVE USERS

Earlier we spoke about the importance of going where your potential audience spends time, such as YouTube and Facebook. They're also on Google+ and by the millions. In fact, Google+ has the second largest active user base of any of the social media sites. And just like Facebook marketing, you can cover a fair amount of ground during your downtime—fifteen to thirty minutes every other day will go a long way.

BUT WHAT ABOUT TWITTER, LINKEDIN, AND INSTAGRAM?

All of these social sites have millions of active users and offer lots of benefits that can help you to push more targeted traffic to your Trust Funnel. I'm currently exploring these sites right now and leveraging them to strengthen my own funnel.

Marketing is a journey, one that never really ends as we continue to push forward, add value, and master the learning process ourselves.

If you are interested in using Instagram rather than Google+, that's awesome. Just take the next step forward and do something. When it comes to online marketing, there are a million ways to find success, and your path may very well be different from mine. You can leverage the *Trust Funnel* principles and strategies to plan your next move.

✔ RECAP:

- All highly successful digital entrepreneurs focus on three key elements in their business: 1) publishing content that adds value (both free and paid), 2) driving traffic to their own Trust Funnel, and 3) building relationships and networks with both customers and peers.

- Social media can be used to address all of these key fundamentals. When moving forward with social media, remember to play by the rules and that people head to these sites to have fun. Thus, your messages should reflect what users want.
- Social media is very synergetic, and as more and more people "like" your messages, pictures, and updates, you'll be able to reach even greater numbers because social media algorithms reward the "like." This is the first step in establishing your funnel and often will lead to trust and financial success.

☜ HOMEWORK

- Choose one social media site to get started with (I chose Facebook).
- Give users what they want, which is to be entertained (follow the golden rule).
- Post a variety of updates; experiment and have fun.
- Brand your business pages and/or channels to match your marketing blog.

CONCLUSION: THE WEALTH WAR CRY

Wow, if you're still here and reading, congrats and know this: You can do anything you set your mind to. You can achieve great things, perhaps more than you have ever dared to dream. It starts with being good to yourself, believing in yourself, surrounding yourself with positive messages and positive people, and taking control of your life. Most important, have clear focus and a definite purpose in what you want to achieve.

Seize opportunity, which is a funny thing and often is close but never in plain sight. Don't expect a welcome invitation, and don't ask if you can enter. Rather, kick that mother down and announce your arrival. I'm talking about taking the bull by the horns and hanging on for dear life as you face your fears head-on. Having done this entrepreneur thing since 2000, I can attest that when I've lived life in this manner, I have always gotten what I set out to achieve. It's never been easy and the journey has always been an interesting one; however, when I played it safe, the rewards were few and far between.

Above all, take care of you. Understand that the journey we face day to day will have challenges. Don't quit three feet from gold; nurture that burning desire for success.

In my experience, these philosophies and this mindset is absolutely necessary to achieve success. Most of the high-level entrepreneurs I know speak of these things. You too can model yourself after success and adopt this very mindset. Remember, success is not found in a plugin, some software code, or even a mentor. It comes from inside you.

I want to leave you with my wealth war cry, which came to me on April 4, 2014, while writing this very book. My war cry hit me like a bolt of hot lightning when I was fully ready to commit to the success I desire, or what I consider my mission in life: to have a positive impact, leave my mark, and inspire, educate, and help others live a life they set out to live.

At first, I considered ending this book with important notes to remember and whatnot. However, as I sat down and started to write this final page, this poured out of me. It's my war cry. It's how I will be living my life as I move forward from this day.

I'd like to share it with you too, and I hope it fills you with strength and energy to crush it online. Oh, and by the way, it's a lot more fun to read this aloud as if you were on a battlefield with a sword in your hand. Don't just read it, but feel it—shout it out from a hilltop. And believe it with every ounce of your being.

The Brian G. Johnson Wealth War Cry

Today I stake my claim!

From this day I will be wealthy in finance, friendship, and life in general.

I will play for all the marbles, and they will be mine!

I will stare down the face of fear as I kick open the door of opportunity and announce my arrival wherever life may take me.

I will let no man tell me otherwise, for it is me and me alone that is in control of my destiny.

I will create a clear and concise plan of action based on my wants and desires.

And each day I will act upon that plan until that which I want has become mine.

Today I stake my claim!

Continue the journey! Access the missing chapter as well as free Trust Funnel training from me, Brian G. Johnson, at:

• • • • • • • • • • • •

Download missing chapter twelve
and access additional training videos at:

TrustFunnel Academy.com/next

Instantly access chapter twelve by entering your name
and awesome email address.

• • • • • • • • • • • •

Peace, love, and happiness. I look forward to finding your Trust Funnel one day in the very near future and remember, you can do anything you set your mind on!

Brian G. Johnson
People **DO NOT** fail at Internet marketing,
they simply **GIVE UP** before the magic happens.

CPSIA information can be obtained at www.ICGtesting.com
Printed in the USA
BVOW04s1042140115

383278BV00001B/1/P